Weapons of the Ancient World

Other titles in this series:

Cassell's Introducing Archaeology Series

Weapons of the Ancient World

RIVKA GONEN

Cassell · London

CASSELL & COMPANY LTD

an imprint of
Cassell & Collier Macmillan Publishers Ltd
35 Red Lion Square, London WC1R 4SG
and at Sydney, Auckland, Toronto, Johannesburg
and an affiliate of The Macmillan Company Inc,
New York

Designed by Ofra Kamar

First published in Great Britain 1975

ISBN 0 304 29338 5

Printed by Peli Press, Ltd., Givataim

PRINTED IN ISRAEL

F. 1274

CONTENTS

INTRODUCTION

1. WHAT ARE WEAPONS?

Weapons are the tools of the warrior on the battlefield. The task of the warrior in employing weapons is twofold: He must attack his enemy, but must also protect himself from that enemy. Thus, the term "weapons" must include the means borne by the warrior both for attack and for defence.

Nature has endowed man, like the other animals, with various natural weapons — the fist, which can deal a stunning blow; the open palm, which can give a shocking slap; and the fingernails and teeth, which can gash deep wounds into the flesh. Such "weapons" served man from the beginning, and they continue to fill certain functions even today in hand-to-hand combat, such as boxing, wrestling and karate. Though suitable for simple man-to-man fighting, they are hardly efficient in man's struggle with larger and stronger beasts. For this he needed auxiliary means — weapons — the earliest of which were unworked stones and clubs of wood; these enabled him to increase the force of his blows and, more important, he could throw them at his quarry, increasing his range of effectiveness. This latter point introduced a new dimension into hunting and warfare. From this point on, offensive weapons were of two major classes: close-range, direct extensions of the human arm; and long-range, stick and stone missiles thrown by the human arm (and later by other means).

When man learned to fashion weapons, these two classes of arms began their true course of development. The pointed hand-axe, and later the stone knife, took over from the fingernails and teeth; stone "points", undoubtedly spearheads fixed at the end of a shaft, permitted stabbing at a range farther away from the body of the user.

The greatest breakthrough in early weaponry came with the development of new means of projecting or shooting missiles. These were simple mechanical means for producing greater energy than that available from human muscle. This invention goes far beyond any normal development from close-range weapons, and represents a milestone in the intellectual advance of man. It necessitated some understanding of the workings of physics and their practical potential.

The earliest complex long-range weapon known to us is the bow. Human figures holding bows are depicted in rock-carvings from the Upper Palaeolithic period (several tens of thousands of years ago), and stone arrowheads can be found scattered over dwelling-sites from this period onward. Of course, we have no precise knowledge of the practical or intellectual stages which produced the bow; but its very invention opened a new page in the story of warfare. Alongside the bow, the sling was used to throw stones; unlike the bow, however, the sling was not in continuous use through the ages, and there is no evidence of its being any further developed. The bow remained pre-eminent among long-range weaponry until the introduction of firearms, only some 600 years ago.

After the bow and sling had served man for many thousands of years, new long-range weapons were developed towards the end of the 1st millennium BC. These were the catapult and ballista, hurling huge arrows and heavy stones respectively, and they greatly increased the range and force of the missiles.

In the realm of defensive weapons, man is not endowed naturally with any protection for his body. His own skin is neither thick nor tough, and it has no continuous, dense hairy covering. Thus, early man had to rely on his own speed and cunning. Actually, the very increase in range of his own weapons was a sort of defensive measure. The shield, helmet and body-armour — all devised clearly for protective reasons — are known only from the beginning of the historical period. But it was possible that some or all of these were in use before our earliest extant sources.

The shield, helmet and body-armour are means of personal protection, providing cover from the offensive weapons of the enemy. But thousands of years ago men built collective means of protection — city-walls around their cities. These, in turn, were countered by the battering-ram — an effective instrument for breaching fortifications. We cannot go here into the interesting subject of the attack on and defence of city fortifications, which would make a book in itself.

Mobility was another essential factor on the battlefield. The most mobile weapon in antiquity, for a period of two thousand years, was the chariot. This weapon demanded not only technical knowledge for building it but also the ability to domesticate and train the proper animals for drawing it. The appearance of the chariot on the battlefield was possible only when these two factors could be teamed together to produce this complex vehicle.

2. DEVELOPMENT OF WEAPONS

Every army continually strives to perfect its arsenal of weapons and to gain an advantage in weaponry over its rivals. It must also watch the development of enemy weaponry and close any gap in sophistication; this can be achieved by devising new defensive measures or by increasing the effectiveness of existing offensive means. Thus, an effective arsenal is balanced dynamically: any step taken by one rival presents the other with a challenge which must be met. This is so today and has been so throughout the history of mankind. Thus, we can trace the measures taken to improve the bow, to give it greater power and range; and in parallel we can see how various armies sought to improve body-armour, in order to reduce the effectiveness of the enemy's archery.

The process of developing weaponry is helped by inventions and discoveries in the various realms of technology and science. One of the important breakthroughs in the manufacture of weapons came when man learned to use metals.

This permitted the making of a wide variety of weapons with sharp points and edges, and brought cutting and stabbing weapons to the forefront. The utilization of metal was gradual: at first, weapons were made in copper, an easily smelted and readily worked metal. But copper is quite soft and weapons made from it tend to bend or break; also they lose their sharpness. Later, man learned to add a small proportion of tin to copper, forming the alloy called bronze; this is much tougher than pure copper and soon replaced it as the principal material for weapons. Indeed, it remained so until the advent of iron-working. Iron itself is quite hard, and this property was further increased when man learned to make various alloys from it. An iron-alloy sword could serve a warrior for his lifetime.

The advance of metallurgy and metalworking was quite slow, as was the entire process of weapon development. Generally, extended periods of stagnation were interrupted only after lengthy accumulation of experience and gradual change. We know of no specific efforts to develop means of warfare prior to the Classical period in Greece. One of the reasons for the slow progress lies in the scarcity of raw materials and in the primitive methods of smelting and working them; further hindrances were provided by national monopolies over the mines, and by the guilds of metal-workers.

After the development of a particular advanced weapon in one place, its spread to other regions was quite slow. Means of transport in the ancient world were slow and rather haphazard; as a result the flow of knowledge from place to place was sporadic. In antiquity, most peoples and states had few economic resources, preventing them from focusing their efforts on the manufacture or purchase of newly developed weapons — again leading to a slower pace of technology. In ancient times most of the population had a low level of technological ability, and thus was often unable to absorb and use new weapons to full advantage. Further, widespread cultural conservatism, even in the leadership, held back the development and introduction of new weapon types.

In this light we can understand why reaction to any new development was slow in coming. We must remember, however, that our knowledge of ancient weapons is far from complete. What may seem to us a gap between the appearance of a weapon and the development of the means for countering it may, in fact, be a mere gap in *our* knowledge. Further archaeological discoveries may well fill in our picture and may destroy misconceptions held concerning the history of weapons.

3. SOURCES FOR THE STUDY OF ANCIENT WEAPONS

There are three principal sources for the study of the weapons of the ancient world — archaeological finds from scientific excavations; ancient monuments (paintings, bas-reliefs and sculptures) showing warriors and their weapons; and ancient literary descriptions. Each of these sources has its strong and weak points.

The archaeological finds are either whole or partial weapons, found mainly in tombs. Such weapons are the prime direct evidence for our subject, but under most conditions the parts made of organic materials — the shafts, handles and bindings — have long since vanished. We generally find only those weapons, or parts of weapons, which were made of stone or metal — sword blades, and the heads of maces, axes, arrows, spears and javelins. These surviving parts merely represent those weapons which were not melted down after breaking or becoming obsolete, and those which were lost on the battlefield. Iron is much more prone to corrosion than are copper and bronze; the number of iron weapons which have survived is thus much smaller than the number of bronze ones.

It should be remembered too, that some of the weapons found in archaeological

A bronze "sickle sword", found in a tomb

were donated to temples, amongst the ruins of which they have been found. But these ceremonial weapons are modelled on the actual weapons of war, and so are of value for our study.

In order to reconstruct details which have been lost to us, we can refer to the many monuments which have survived from antiquity. Each of the major nations of ancient times perpetuated its wars in its own typical style. The Sumerians, earliest of the peoples inhabiting southern Mesopotamia, left numerous artistic objects such as inlays, carved stoneware and seals, depicting scenes of worship, ceremony and war. The kings and nobles of Egypt have left a colourful series of tomb-paintings in which various facets of life are depicted. They are highly informative on the military campaigns and the weapons used by Egyptian troops in the various periods. The kings of Egypt perpetuated their deeds of valour also in vast temple reliefs. The kings of Assyria, who ruled over one of the most aggressive peoples in antiquity, ornamented the walls of their huge palaces with rows of reliefs depicting their deeds; war obviously occupies a prominent place here, and Assyrian methods and weapons of war are thus among the best documented from ancient times. This plethora of material from ancient monuments in Egypt and Assyria is matched in Greece

excavations were more ceremonial than military. It cannot be assumed that warriors, even kings, marched to the field of battle with axes or daggers of pure gold, inlaid with precious stones. Such weapons were for display and were presented as gifts to rulers who would have them placed in their tombs; or they

A wall relief depicting the siege of the town of Lachish from the palace of Sennacherib, King of Assyria, at Nineveh

B.M.

by an amazingly rich legacy of depictions on pottery vessels, a prime source on weapons and warfare among the Greeks. The rulers of Rome also depicted their wars and victories in monumental reliefs, mainly on huge columns and triumphal arches built in public places throughout their empire.

These numerous monuments represent an almost inexhaustible source for the study of weapons and the nature of war in many periods. Their disadvantage lies in their mostly two-dimensional nature and in artistic conventions which veil true dimensions and methods of employing the more complex of the weapons, such as the battering-ram, ballista and catapult. Complementary material can be found among literary sources, which describe both the weapons themselves and, especially, the manner in which they were employed. Unfortunately, the writings which have survived are never plentiful, and the earlier the period the scarcer they are. Often only a very brief description of some decisive battle appears, usually only an outline of the basic course of events. Rarely are the weapons named. From the Hellenistic and Roman periods onward, the literary sources, both whole and fragmentary,

increase considerably, and for such periods it is possible even to analyse the overall military set-up, revealing a reasonably complete picture of the various elements forming it.

Still lacking much essential material, we know little of the origins of the various types of weapons, of their exact construction or of their evolution at different times and places.

*

The weapons used by ancient warriors are only a part of the overall subject of war in antiquity. Their role in achieving victory was important but not always decisive.

Within the strict limits of our subject, we shall deal here with the description and development of the various tools of war. The five sections cover: (a) short-range weapons, with which the enemy was struck at close quarters — the mace, axe, dagger, sword and spear (including the javelin); (b) long-range weapons, shot at the enemy from some distance — the bow, sling, catapult and ballista; (c) protective armour — shield, helmet and coat of mail or cuirass; and (d) chariots, as the means for transporting the warrior to and in battle.

I SHORT-RANGE WEAPONS

Short-range weapons fulfil three principal functions: striking, cutting and piercing — each function displaying a developmental history of its own. Thus, the mace deals a crushing blow to the head or arms; some weapons (e.g., axes and most swords) slash or hack; and others (javelin, spear and some swords) pierce the body.

Generally speaking, the invention or improvement of one type of weapon reduced the reliance upon another. The cutting axe replaced the crushing mace, and the sword superseded the axe, as both a cutting weapon and a thrusting one, in hand-to-hand combat. Such short-range weapons are all made of two elements. The "blade", which cuts or pierces, is generally quite small; early smiths could easily cast such weapons in metal in spite of their limited metallurgical knowledge. The metal blade was attached to a handle or shaft of wood. An exception was the sword, in which the blade was often as long as or longer than the handle, so that its casting and forging were more complex than with any other of the short-range

weapons. Attaching the metal blade to the wooden handle or shaft was a major problem in all these weapons, and several solutions were found. One basic way of joining the two elements was by means of a tang — a tapered projection at the base of the blade, which was inserted into a hole or slot in the wood; this was then bound and probably glued fast. A rather later method of attaching blades was by means of a tubular extension at the base of the blade, into which the wooden shaft was inserted. Such a socket was more efficient for most types of weapons, and eventually it replaced the tang almost entirely.

1. MACE

The mace, one of the earliest common forms of weapon, was intended to inflict a crushing blow upon the victim. Wooden clubs fill the same function and no doubt were the prototype of the mace; indeed, staves have been used by shepherds and peasants in all periods. It was found that a thickened, heavy head increased the force of the blow,

Bronze maceheads from Israel, 4th millennium BC

and thus branches were selected with part of the trunk still attached, to provide a natural head. Heavy sticks were also carved so as to leave a thickened head on a slender, more convenient shaft. All-wooden clubs were common among primitive peoples throughout the world.

In the Ancient Near East, a focal point of early technological and cultural development, the mace was improved by making it in two parts — a wooden handle and a head of some heavier material. Stone and copper mace-heads appear in the Ancient Near East as early as the 4th millennium BC. Their advantage over the one-piece wooden club was considerable, though it was difficult to join the two parts, made of different materials, in such a manner that the head would not fly loose even during the heaviest of blows. In all known examples of mace-heads this was overcome by making a round socket in the head, into which the wooden handle was inserted. The wooden handles have perished but we may assume that they were of the same diameter as the sockets and fitted tightly within them. The bond was further strengthened by tapering the socket, to prevent the head from flying off during the stroke. Some mace-heads have survived with carved ornamentation in relief, often in a cross pattern, possibly an imitation of the thong binding the head to the handle.

The mace was not equally popular throughout the Ancient Near East. The Egyptians and their Canaanite neighbours preferred it and utilized it to great advantage against their enemies. Many mace-heads have been found in Egypt and Canaan, dating to the period between the mid 4th and the mid 3rd millennia BC. In Mesopotamia, however, the mace is more rare. Here we have an early instance of the interaction of offensive and defensive weapons. The methods of fighting among the Sumerians, the early inhabitants of Mesopotamia, were much more advanced than those of the Egyptians. The Sumerians wore helmets as early as the first half of the 3rd millennium BC, and the blunt maces apparently proved ineffective against them. Though some mace-heads have been found in Mesopotamia, they are carved and ornamental, and thus probably of ceremonial nature, survivals from the pre-helmet era. In extant Sumerian art, the mace is rarely found in depictions of warfare.

When the mace was found ineffective, no attempt was made to improve its form. From start to finish, this weapon

Narmer, King of Egypt, smashing the heads of enemies with a mace, depicted on a stone palette

remained the same, with essentially no history of development or improvement. Only in Egypt was an attempt made to give the mace a cutting action; this new form had a discoid head with a sharpened edge, but it too was soon replaced. Thus even in Egypt the mace lost its supremacy during the 3rd millennium BC, never again to regain it in warfare in the Ancient Near East.

A significant improvement in the effectiveness of the mace appeared only in a much later period. This was the addition of spikes on the head, enabling it to pierce helmet and body-armour. These protective devices had previously been the major counter to the mace. These studded maces came to the fore as important and dangerous weapons on the battlefield after an absence of several thousand years, and were common in Europe and Asia from the Middle Ages onward. This new form remained in use as long as short-range combat between heavily armoured warriors was the normal procedure of battle.

The Egyptian god Horus holding a mace symbolic of victory, depicted on the chariot of Thutmes IV

The mace has remained among the common symbols of authority, from ancient times to the present. In ancient Egypt it appeared in the hands of kings and gods as the weapon of victory on the battlefield and, hence, the symbol of might and authority. Even today, it preserves its ceremonial character in the sceptres and batons of kings and field-marshals, which are little more than sophisticated forms of the ancient mace.

2. AXE

The drawback of the mace was its inability to cut and pierce the body or split the helmet and armour worn by the enemy. The axe — unlike the mace, from which it may well have developed — overcame this difficulty. Its sharp edge was intended primarily to cut and slash the unprotected body of the victim. In modified form it could even break through a helmet or metal body-armour.

As long as warriors entered the field of battle without body-armour, the principal function of the axe was to hack and slash. With the introduction of the metal helmet and armour, however, the axe was improved to overcome them. This difference in function led to a decided change in form: the cutting axe has a broad blade, whereas the piercing axe is narrow, focusing its impact upon a small spot in the victim's armour. The intended function of the axe — whether cutting or piercing — influenced not only its shape but also the manner in which the head was hafted. We have already seen the problem of joining parts made of different materials, and the various solutions aimed at preventing the metal part from loosening during the swing or on impact. The different attempts to develop an efficient join led to two principal types here too: tang and socket. In tanged axes, the blade is thin at the joint with the handle; the socketed axe, in contrast, has quite a thick blade towards the handle end, so as to enclose the socket.

There is a general correspondence between the shape of the axe blade and the type of joint with the handle. The broad-bladed cutting axes are usually hafted by means of tangs, whereas the narrow-bladed piercing axes are usually socketed. The reasoning behind this may be that, in penetrating metal armour, the joint must bear up to a much heavier shock, even though having the socket within the blade involved a technically complex casting. In cutting axes, however, where the shock was considerably less, the hafting could be much simpler.

A broad cutting axe used against an unarmoured enemy, on an Egyptian relief of the 3rd millennium BC

Thutmes IV, King of Egypt, in his battle chariot; note the narrow-bladed, tanged axe

Both principal types of axe, cutting and piercing, as well as both methods of hafting, are found at the very beginning of the historical period. In the mountainous regions to the north and east of Mesopotamia (modern Turkey and Iran) and in Mesopotamia proper — regions already outstanding in early times for their metal-working and weaponry — socketed piercing axes appear in the 3rd millennium BC. This type of axe apparently developed in reaction to the introduction of the metal helmet. There is evidence of such helmets in the early Sumerian cities (see below). In contrast, in Egypt — a most conservative country as far as armament was concerned — the tanged cutting axe remained standard for many centuries. In Egypt and Canaan, various solutions were found for the problem of hafting.

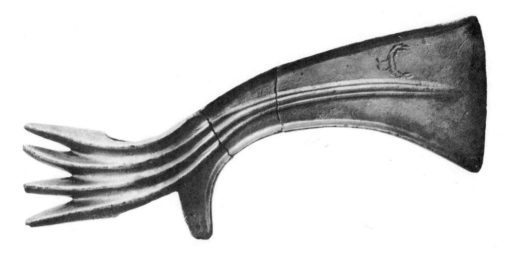

A bronze socketed piercing axe from Beth-Shean

The continued use of the tanged axe stems from the fact that Egypt and her adjacent enemies never really came to utilize the helmet or body-armour of any type, relying on a hand-held shield for personal protection. Under these circumstances, there was no real need for a piercing axe. Even when the Egyptians came to adopt more advanced methods of warfare, upon coming up against populations which excelled in "modern" forms of warfare and weaponry — around the mid 2nd millennium BC — they did little to change the technology of their axes. Though they gradually manufactured axes which were increasingly narrower, reaching the point where they could function as piercing axes, the hafting generally continued to be tanged.

With the spread of body armour and especially the helmet, the cutting axe declined in favour of the piercing axe. A contributory factor in this process was that the function of cutting or slashing was not the attribute of the axe alone, but could be done also by the sword. The wavering ascendancy of hacking axe and cutting sword can be seen throughout the development of both types of weapon. In the early period the axe was predominant, with a fairly small metal head. The early smith could make quite complex axeheads even with simple raw materials and his limited technical knowledge. With the development of better techniques, the sword came to the fore as the prime cutting weapon. Later, towards the end of the 2nd millennium BC, the axe fell out of use altogether on the battlefields of the Ancient Near East. From this time on, fine swords were cast and forged, good for stabbing and hacking alike, and the role of the axe as a compromise between mace and sword came to an end.

Though the axe had generally gone out of use, it remained a popular weapon among the marginal peoples and tribes of the region. In the Graeco-Roman world, the battle-axe was never used, though other European peoples, north of the Alps, used it for a lengthy period. The axes of the tribes of Luristan in Iran are famous for their beauty and fine quality, as are the other bronze weapons and utensils from that land. The axes of the Scythian and Cimmerian tribes — peoples of the southern Steppes — are equally outstanding. The combination of "Scythian" bow for long range and battle-axe for short range is typical of these tribes.

The wide variety of potential uses of the axe made it a most popular weapon in the Ancient Near East. It appears in various regions at various periods in a multitude of forms: besides battle-axes for hand-to-hand combat, there were light axes especially balanced for throwing, placing them in the category of medium-range and long-range weapons. We also know of axes so heavy that both hands were required to wield them.

Most axes had just one cutting edge, though the double axe was common at times. The island of Crete was famous for its double-axe, which was more ceremonial and ritual than for war. In antiquity there were also axes of precious metals, presented to temples as offerings, or with artistic ornamentation of the highest quality, for the parade use of rulers and nobility. One of the most famous symbols of rule was the Roman *fasces,* actually a bundle of rods, sometimes shown bound around the handle of an axe. This weapon was borne by a special functionary before the highest officials of Rome. The bundle of rods symbolized the right to inflict a judicial beating, while the axe represented the power over life and death. The *fasces* was adopted by Mussolini and his adherents as their symbol, hence the name "Fascists".

3. SWORD AND DAGGER

Hand-to-hand combat of old is often conceived of as duels between swordsmen. This picture is hardly accurate as regards the earlier periods of history. The reason for the relatively late development of the sword is inherent in its very form and in the technical difficulties of its manufacture. In most ancient weapons, the metal blade was small in proportion to the whole, and was set on a wooden shaft or handle; the opposite is true of the sword, in which the metal blade comprises most of the length and the hilt, of such materials as wood or bone, was relatively small. The structure of the sword presented several technical difficulties. As long as a really hard metal was lacking, the armourer was unable to forge an efficient sword, and the early bronze swords were more like daggers in form. A long, narrow blade made of even the hardest copper or bronze would break during use. Only with metallurgical developments — especially the advance in working iron — was it possible to make fighting swords of any reliability.

Two actions can be effected with the sword: stabbing and cutting. This lead to the evolution of two major forms, what we today would call the rapier for thrusting, and the sabre for cutting. The sharp-pointed rapier must be light and as thin and narrow as possible: its centre of gravity should be close to the hilt, to facilitate holding the tip high. Thus, the rapier is heavier near the hilt and tapers down to the tip. In contrast, the function of the sabre calls for a heavy blade, with a centre of gravity towards the point, to lend weight to the blow. The sabre, unlike the rapier, can be of many forms — straight or curved, concave or convex, one- or two-

edged. Sabres with one convex edge are particularly efficient for slashing — drawing the entire blade across the cut, making an especially long wound. In spite of the basic differences in the forms of these two main types of sword, some attempts were made to combine both functions in a single weapon. This led to an intermediate form, which could be produced successfully only by the most skilled armourers, able to find the right compromise. These dual-purpose swords were so difficult to manufacture that two separate swords were generally preferred.

The forms of the sword at various periods are indicative of the search for more efficient weapons. In turn, the oscillations in preference between rapier and sabre reflect the technical achievements of the various periods — as well as the position of the sword relative to the other weapons used, especially the battle-axe and spear. The rapier is the ideal companion to the broad-axe; when proper methods of making sabres were developed, the axe diminished in importance. The spear, when used for stabbing at close range, reduced the need for the long rapier, further promoting the development of the sabre.

At the base of the sword family tree lies the short dagger. This weapon, not exceeding a foot in length, had a simple function. The sharp-tipped dagger blade was made of bronze, with several perforations at the base for the rivets holding it to the wooden or bone hilt. This simple form of join was gradually improved by increasing the length of the base till an actual tang had developed. Daggers of this type were in widespread use throughout the Ancient Near East in the 3rd millennium and the first half of the 2nd millennium BC, and numerous examples have been found in archaeological excavations. In Mesopotamia, splendid daggers were discovered in the royal Sumerian tombs; several of these are of gold, with hilts of semi-precious stones or ivory; their finely wrought gold sheaths are also most impressive. It is interesting to note that, in spite of the relative abundance of daggers among the archaeological finds, they do not appear on any of the monuments of either Egypt or Mesopotamia. This is probably indicative of the relative unimportance of this weapon in early warfare.

A decided improvement in daggers came when armourers began casting blade and hilt in one piece. This overcame the major problem of joining the two parts, and led to the possibility of a sword with the strength required for a hacking function — till then reserved for the axe. This new advantage led to the "sickle-sword" (which, unlike a true sickle, was sharp on the convex, outer edge of the blade). The sickle-sword was actually a sort of cross between sword and axe, and was the archetype of the scimitars so popular in the East for thousands of years. It was commonly used in Egypt. Anatolia and the regions in between during much of the 2nd millennium BC. At first its hilt was twice as long as the blade – more axe than sword: but slowly the proportions changed and the blade became longer.

During the 2nd millennium BC, while in the East the sickle-sword was used for cutting and the dagger for stabbing, in Greece we find a very long sword (occasionally more than three feet long!) for thrusting alone. This represents the first and only true rapier of antiquity. Such swords have been found in considerable numbers in the Shaft Tombs at Mycenae, royal tombs of the 16th century BC. Long rapiers were apparently not an original Greek development, but originated in the technology of the bronze-workers of Crete. The enormous technical skill required for their manufacture could hardly have been justified by their effectiveness in battle: they were very heavy and brittle, and the tang joining blade and hilt was quite thin. To overcome the weaknesses of the long rapier, the Mycenaean armourers both reduced the length and improved the manner of hafting, by

Rameses III, King of Egypt, brandishing a "sickle-sword"

"Sea-people" mercenaries using long straight swords, fighting alongside Egyptian soldiers using "sickle-swords". A relief depicting Rameses III's war against the Libyans, 13th century BC

making the tang thicker and adding flanking lugs as guards for the hand. This gave birth to the "horned" and cross-shaped swords — popular, common forms in widespread areas from the Danube region to Israel.

The narrow rapier type did not long survive, and was replaced by a sword originating in Eastern Europe, especially in the region known today as Hungary. Here the armourers achieved a high level of metal-working and in the 2nd millennium BC they were already producing effective swords of one piece. These straight swords, two-edged and with a stabbing point, are the earliest dual-purpose swords known. They are the first link in a long series of large, dual-purpose swords for which Europe was famous for many centuries. The armourers of Bronze Age Greece adopted this efficient sword, producing it as early as the 14th century BC. In this same period, Greece and the Aegean region began forging links with the East;

at first these were commercial ties, but soon Egypt was hiring mercenaries from among the "Sea Peoples" from the west. Later, in the 12th century BC, waves of migrants from the Aegean region, including the Philistines, began arriving on the eastern shores of the Mediterranean Sea. These "Sea Peoples" brought with them their advanced metallurgical technology, which they derived from the peoples of Eastern Europe. Under this influence the first dual-purpose swords were made in the East, long-bladed (about 30 inches), two-edged and pointed. From this time on the sickle-sword disappears, for its only role as a hacking sword had become superfluous.

But even this fine sword, like most dual-purpose weapons, was short-lived. The armies of Greece in the 1st millennium BC favoured the spear for stabbing, rather than the sword, and gave it preference in their warfare. No longer was the long rapier needed,

A red-figured Greek amphora depicting a Greek warrior with spear and *hoplon* shield, attacking a Persian armed with composite bow and *kyris* sword and the sword of the Greek warrior was greatly shortened. Around the 5th century BC a new type of sword came into use in Greece, unknown in Europe till then. This was a slightly curved blade with a single edge — used solely for cutting. This is assumed to be the *kopis* of the Greek literary sources, introduced following contact with the East, especially Persia. This sabre was in effect a late version of the early sickle-sword. On the painted Greek vases we can see this new sabre, raised over the left shoulder, above the head, preparatory to the swing. The *kopis* served as an auxiliary weapon after the spear was lost or broken, or in very close combat. A famous instance of abandoning spear for sword was the fatal struggle of the Spartans under Leonidas in the final phase of the battle at Thermopylae. The *kopis* was used also by the Macedonian army, and the historian Arrian relates that during the battle of Granicus, Cleitus hacked off the entire arm of a Persian commander who was about to fell Alexander the Great.

The tradition of large, heavy swords continued among the tribes of Europe into the Roman period (and even much later), and the Romans derived their sword from this same source. The *gladius,* the famous sword of the Roman legions, was also known as the "Spanish sword", probably because it was

The so-called *gladius* of the Roman emperor Tiberius

A relief on a Roman sarcophagus; note how the cutting sword is manipulated.

B.M.

adopted after contact with the tribes of Iberia. The *gladius,* also used of course in the gladiatorial bouts, was basically a very efficient sabre. Its blade was about two feet long and some two inches wide. The edges were straight and parallel, tapering to a point only at the end. This sword, made of iron from Spain, was outstanding for its light weight and fine balance. The tang ran through the entire hilt, thus ensuring a proper join. The *gladius* was carried by the Roman legionary in a wooden scabbard worn on the right side (rather than on the more usual left); it was drawn out with an upward movement and brought down on the victim with a force sufficient to split his body-armour. When held low, it could also serve for thrusting.

Auxiliary troops in the Roman army, recruited from among the various tribes, introduced the *spatha,* a long sabre, the direct descendant of the long sword of old. The *spatha* was longer (about 30 inches) and thinner than the *gladius* of the legionary. Eventually, the *spatha* came to replace the *gladius* as the principal sword of the Roman army.

The heavy, straight sword — used primarily for cutting but also for stabbing in time of need — continued to be used in Europe for hundreds of years. In the East, the homeland of the sickle-sword and the *kopis,* the tradition of curved sabres lived on till modern times.

4. SPEAR AND JAVELIN

The spear and the javelin bridge the gap between short-range weapons — which remain in the hands of the warrior throughout the battle — and long-range weapons, shot or thrown from a distance.

The spear and the javelin are very similar in form; both have a long wooden shaft with a pointed head at one end, normally made of metal. But the two weapons are used in an entirely different manner: the spear is used to stab and thrust at close quarters, while the javelin is thrown at the enemy at medium range. The javelin differs from the other long-range weapons in that it is propelled entirely by the direct force of the thrower; no artificial means are used to concentrate the energy involved, as in the sling or bow. In this it is a very simple weapon, like the close-range weapons.

These two weapons undoubtedly stem from a pointed stick, used by primitive man in hunting and war from earliest times. The tips of such wooden spears were hardened by fire, as was still done, for instance, by some Germanic tribes in Roman times. The Greek word for a spear — *dory* — literally means a tree or stem, revealing the origin of this weapon.

As with the other weapons described above, the wooden shafts of spears and javelins have not generally been preserved. What archaeological excavations have revealed is a series of metal heads of varying sizes and shapes. The main difficulty is distinguishing between spear-heads and javelin-heads, for they are quite similar. The chief criterion seems to be size: the spear-head, intended to pierce at close range, was longer and heavier, while the javelin, thrown from a distance, had a shorter and lighter head. But between the larger blades, undoubtedly spear-heads, and the smaller ones, which are surely from javelins, there are numerous heads which are difficult to classify.

Another distinction between spear-heads and javelin-heads may lie in the proportion between the actual blade and the tang or socket. The difference between the tang or socket of the spear and that of the javelin stems from the difference in their use. To ensure stable flight, the centre of gravity of the javelin had to be close to the middle of the shaft. Thus, the tangs (and later sockets) were made quite long. In contrast, the optimum centre of gravity for the spear, to facilitate thrusting at close-range, was farther forward, near the point, and the tang or socket could be shorter and heavier. The proportions of the two parts of the head — blade and tang or socket — on the two weapons are exactly opposite; javelin, short blade, long tang or socket, spear, long blade, short tang or socket.

Though distinguishing between spear- and javelin-heads is often difficult among the archaeological finds, their different functions and methods of employment are depicted quite clearly on the many monuments surviving from antiquity.

a. Spear

Ancient monuments reveal the important part played by the spear as a close-range weapon of attack. The spear, meant for piercing, could perform a task which the sword was to take over only after a very long time. As the spear had a relatively small metal head attached to a long wooden shaft, it was much easier to manufacture than the sword, and because of its weight it could deal a heavy, piercing blow. Thus, it was a prime offensive weapon, and special tactics were evolved for it in armies which did not extensively employ the bow, preferring to fight at close quarters.

In armies utilizing the bow, spearmen followed the archers and comprised the main attacking force, going into action after a volley of arrows had softened enemy resistance.

On the very earliest monuments there is evidence for the common use of the spear. It first appears as a hunter's weapon: on the "Hunters' Palette", made in Egypt around 3000 BC, hunters are shown bearing spears which are more than a man's height. The lion-hunter depicted on the stela from Warka in Mesopotamia, also from about 3000 BC, has pierced the lion with a long spear. Lion-hunting with a spear at close range, which requires no little courage, was a favourite pastime in Mesopotamia throughout early history, from the early Sumerians of the 3rd millennium BC down to the Assyrian kings of the 1st millennium BC.

The Egyptians did not favour fighting with the spear. After the earliest period, as represented by the "Hunters' Palette", there is no evidence for the use of the spear there for some 1000 years. In contrast, the Sumerians were quick to appreciate the potential of the spear, and developed special troops of spearmen to exploit it to the full. In Greece some 2000 years later, a special formation of spearmen was again developed, known as the "phalanx"; this term is now applied in describing even the much

"The Hunters' Palette", 4th millennium BC, showing a variety of weapons used by ancient Egyptians; note the simple bow, spear and mace   B.M.

earlier Sumerian phenomenon. The principle of the phalanx lies in its dense rows of shield-bearing spearmen, forming a living wall from which a forest of spears projected. The organized advance of the phalanx, at a run, was almost impossible to stop. The fallen enemy lying at the feet of the Sumerian phalanx well demonstrates the crushing effectiveness of such an attack. This formation, acting as a single, coordinated body, required the absolute discipline of individual warriors. Each soldier was dependent upon the courage of his fellows. Thus, it is no wonder that this device was developed in the city-states of both Sumeria and Greece. In both cases, rule was based on the city unit, in which the army was a citizens' army. In the large kingdoms of the Ancient Near East, where armies were made up mainly of mercenaries, there was little possibility of achieving the structure of the phalanx. In the Egyptian army, from the New Kingdom onward, and especially in the Assyrian Empire, there were corps of spearmen, representing the main striking force, but they operated in rather open formations, hardly comparable with the compactness of the phalanx.

In the Aegean world, the spear was the most popular weapon. At Mycenae it appears from the 16th century BC on, used by infantry and chariotry alike, and it was the weapon of the "heroes" of the period, as described in the Homeric poems. The heavy spear of Achilles was greatly glorified and this hero often used it as a javelin. The most highly respected epithet of the Homeric hero was "famous in the use of the spear".

The Sumerian "phalanx" of King Eanatum   β.Μ.

The heyday of the spear came with the development of the hoplite, the heavy infantryman of the Greek city-states (named after his large, round shield, the *hoplon*). His main weapon of attack was the long spear. Phalanges formed of hoplites comprised the city-armies of Classical Greece; indeed, the Greek victory in the Persian Wars was ascribed by Aeschylus to the victory of the spear over the bow. The phalanx ideally functioned on flat, open ground, for other terrain could easily bring about the loosening of the formation.

The spearmen of Sargon, King of Assyria, beneath the walls of the besieged city

The most famous phalanx of antiquity was that developed by Philip II of Macedonia and his son Alexander the Great. The Macedonian army had units of foreign mercenaries, but the troops forming the phalanx were always drawn from loyal, trusted subjects. The weapon of the Macedonian phalanx was an especially long spear known as the *sarissa*. There is conflicting evidence in the literary sources as to the form, dimensions and precise use of this weapon, and since no example has

survived, it cannot be reconstructed. One source makes it some 20 feet long, while another would have it about 25 feet. Polybius, the second-century BC historian, notes that in his day the standard length of the *sarissa* was about 22 feet. This lengthy weapon was undoubtedly quite heavy, and was probably rather unwieldy. It can also be assumed that its metal blade was not large. Polybius describes the operation of the Macedonian phalanx; this formation was somewhat more open than its clas-

The famous Greek "Chigi Vase" depicting a phalanx of hoplates

A mosaic floor from Pompeii, depicting the Battle of Issus, with Alexander the Great *(left)* and Darius, King of Persia. Note the long *sarissa*.

sical predecessor, and the distance between each hoplite and his neighbour was about a yard. The *sarissa* was held in both hands, close to the butt, enabling the spearheads of the first four or five rows to project forward before the phalanx. The spears of the rear rows were raised above the heads of the front rows.

The Romans adapted the Greek phalanx to their own needs. The im-portance of the spear is indicated by the fact that loss of his spear was considered the greatest disgrace a Roman soldier could incur. The phalanx was soon abandoned, after the Celtic tribes penetrated into central Italy in 370 BC, conquering even Rome. The Celts were highly mobile and lightly armed, in direct contrast to the plodding Roman hoplites. The lessons taught by the Celtic invasion brought about a reorganization of the Roman battle-line into smaller, more flexible units. The role of the spear did not come to an end, however, in the Roman army. The *hasta,* a spear with broad head, was widely used by both Roman legionaries and auxiliary troops.

The spear also held an important position in chariot warfare, and later in mounted combat. Cavalry spears were generally longer than those of the infantry.

b. Javelin

The javelin, too, has a long and varied history. Unlike the spear, it was never developed as a principal means of warfare; javelin-throwers were integrated within the general array of medium- and long-range troops, alongside the slingers and archers. They were equipped with several javelins apiece, carried either in the hands or in a large quiver. The javelin quiver was often part of the equipment of the battle chariot, as can be seen on the early wagons of the Sumerians, as well as on the faster chariots of the Egyptians and Assyrians in the 2nd and 1st millennia BC. With the advent of true cavalry, the javelin found a new application, and it became one of the ordinary weapons of the horseman ever since.

It is of interest to note the mutual relationship between the javelin and the bow. The javelin is of particular importance in those cultures or periods where the bow was little used. With the development of the stronger forms of bow, however, resulting in increased ranges, the javelin went into eclipse. Thus, in the excavations at Lachish in Israel, which underwent a siege by the Assyrian army around 700 BC, only two javelin-heads were found, as against large quantities of arrow-heads. This can readily be understood when we remember that the composite bow was the prime long-range weapon employed by the Assyrian army.

Several javelin types are noteworthy. In the Mycenaean period, the Greeks increased the range of their javelins by appending a special loop near the middle of the shaft; the thrower would insert the index and middle fingers through the loop and grasp the shaft with the other fingers. It has been suggested that the javelin of Goliath the Philistine, described as "like a weaver's beam" (I Samuel, xvii, 7), was of this latter type; the biblical author, who had no ready term for such a javelin, compared the shaft with its loop to part of a loom, the shaft bearing the looped heddles which separate the threads of the warp.

A unique type of javelin, the *pilum,* was the principal long-range missile of the Roman legionary. The overall length

The "Warrior's Vase", depicting Mycenaean soldiers with large spears, round shields, horned helmets and leather body armour

of the *pilum* was about 10 feet, with a blade of about 30 inches, a socket of about 30 inches and a wooden shaft of some 5 feet. Thus, its centre of gravity was at the socket and this balance insured an increased range. The structure of the head of the *pilum* was unusual and differed from the other sorts of javelinheads; it was made in two parts, with a small blade of forged iron (some 4 inches), and a narrow round shaft of softer iron, to which the socket was joined. The *pilum* thus had considerable power of penetration: when it hit its target, the soft iron shaft would bend near the blade from the weight of the wooden shaft. The wounded victim could not free himself or his shield, if it had been

hit. This peculiar feature of the *pilum* is described accurately and vividly by Julius Caesar in his book on the Gallic Wars. It was after discharging the *pilum* that the Roman legionary would draw his sword and rush the enemy.

Right: Socketed bronze axes from Luristan

Overleaf left and right: "the Standard of Ur",
· an inlayed plaque depicting the Sumerian army in battle array

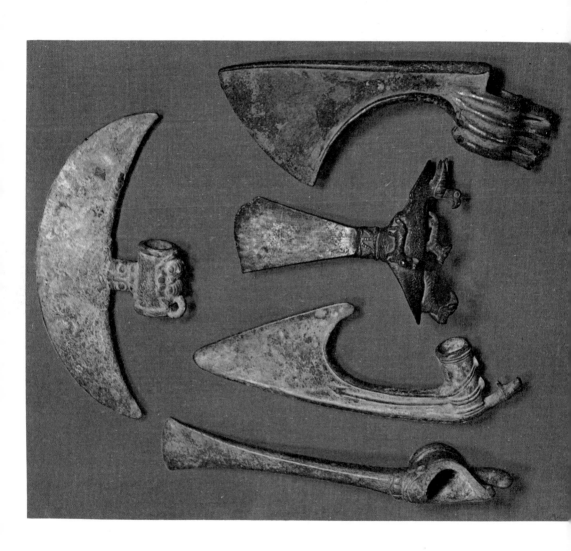

II LONG-RANGE WEAPONS

In antiquity, long-range weapons were intended to inflict casualties on the enemy from afar by means of stones or arrows. The simplest weapon for hurling a stone is the sling, while the primary weapon for shooting arrows is the bow. In the Hellenistic period (from the 4th century BC on) these were supplemented by a crossbow, the catapult and the ballista, all of which increased the range and (especially the latter two) the weight of the missile or projectile to be shot.

Long-range weapons are more sophisticated than close-range weapons in that they utilize energy beyond that generated by unassisted human muscle. The sling utilizes the centrifugal force of circular motion, while the bow, crossbow, catapult and ballista utilize potential energy stored in elastic materials under tension. By using long-range weapons, it was possible to hurt the enemy while still out of range of his javelins or hand-thrown missiles, and even avoid hand-to-hand combat in which the mace, axe, sword and spear came into play. Thus, for instance,

David was able to defeat Goliath in their famous duel; the Bible relates that Goliath "had a helmet of brass upon his head, and he was armed with a coat of mail. And he had greaves of brass upon his legs, and a javelin of brass between his shoulders. And the staff of his spear was like a weaver's beam ... and one bearing a shield went before him" (I Samuel, xvii, 5–7). Thus, Goliath's close and medium range weapons were useless against David's sling-stones. The sling, though a very simple weapon, enabled him to fling the stone very fast over a considerable distance, and hit his enemy before Goliath could put his own weapons into play.

Improvements in long-range weapons generally sought to increase their effective range, whether shooting a stone or an arrow. This development took place, first and foremost, by improving the basic structure of the weapons. In describing them, we shall proceed from the simple to the complex – from the sling to the catapult and ballista.

Left: Daggers and sheaths of Tut-ankh-amun, King of Egypt (all of gold except the iron blade of the dagger on left)

1. SLING

The sling is popularly associated with shepherds rather than with soldiers. Indeed, the combination of club or mace, for close range, and sling, for long range, is typical of shepherds' and peasants' weapons throughout history. The victory of David the shepherd over Goliath the warrior proves the efficiency of the sling when properly handled, and it is surprising that its use was not more widespread in antiquity.

This weapon is made up of two parts; a leather or heavy cloth "pocket" with two cords or thongs for swinging it; and a stone — the missile. The necessary raw materials and technical knowledge required for making the sling are readily available; no special knowledge was needed, and anyone could make one for himself. Using the sling, however, requires considerable practice and skill. A stone was placed in the pocket and then swung round and round above the head; when sufficient centrifugal force had been generated, one of the thongs was released, discharging the stone at a high speed towards its distant target. This weapon, simple as it is, is one of the foremost long-range weapons. In contrast, the sword, axe or spear are relatively difficult to manufacture, but very simple in their use. No ancient slings have survived, nor can early sling-stones be identified as such, for at least till the middle of the 1st century BC they were taken entirely from nature. Thus, we must rely upon depictions on monuments and in literary sources in determining the place of the sling among ancient weaponry. There is no extant evidence of its use in the 3rd millennium BC. It first appears in a siege scene in an Egyptian tomb of the 20th century BC. Some 1000 years later the sling appears again, on a basalt relief from Tell Halaf (Gozan) in northwestern Mesopotamia. Three centuries later slings were in action in the siege of Lachish in Judah by the Assyrian army of Sennacherib. It appears that the sling, operated by troops of slingers alongside archers, was especially effective in siege warfare. The high trajectory of the sling-stone enabled it to clear the ramparts and hit within the city.

The Greek world, too, has left us with little data on the use of the sling in war. Throughout the Mycenaean period, the sling seems to have been in use, though only sporadically. From the Classical period on, warriors from the islands of Crete and Rhodes were noted for their skill as slingers; they served as mercenaries in the armies of the Greek city-states and, later, in the Macedonian army and the armies of the Hellenistic kingdoms. From this time on, the effectiveness of the sling was increased by

Slingers in the army of Sennacherib, King of Assyria B.M.

making sling-stones of lead. Xenophon's *Anabasis*, describing the return of 10,000 Greek mercenaries from Mesopotamia, relates that the effective range of such lead sling-stones was twice that of stone ones. The best Rhodian slingers could achieve a range outdistancing even most archers. In the ruins of Olynthus in northern Greece — which surrendered to Philip II of Macedonia after a siege in 348 BC — archaeologists have found lead sling-stones which had been shot into the city by the besieging Macedonian army. Some of them bear inscriptions, such as the name of Philip, and the names of others of his commanders, or sarcastic taunts such as "a nasty gift".

2. BOW

Unlike the sling, which was only sporadically used in warfare, the bow remained the most effective long-range weapon from its first appearance till the introduction of firearms. The bow is a device for shooting arrows at a far-off enemy. To realize this aim, the bow utilizes energy stored within it. When the drawn string is released, this stored energy is discharged — converted into motion and transferred to the arrow, causing it to fly through the air and strike its target. Thus the bow is inherently a much more complex weapon than the mace, axe or sword, which derive their force directly from the arm of the warrior. After the invention of the bow, armies always attempted to improve it in various ways, constantly seeking to increase its range. The army with the greater range in archery had a very decided advantage on the battlefield; its troops could open effective action while still out of danger, beyond the range of the enemy's arrows. The developed bow, especially one operated upon a movable platform such as a chariot or a horse, was a most decisive weapon in many a battle and led to more than one major change in history.

a. Operation of the Bow

The bow is constructed of two basic elements — the bow proper and the string, drawn taut to send the arrow on its flight. The bow is held in the left hand by a grip at its middle, and the string is drawn back with the right hand, stretching from the two tips of the bow. The arrow rests upon the left fist, which is closed around the grip; its tail is held by the fingers of the right hand, up against the string.

The further the bowstring is drawn, the greater the energy behind it, and thus also the driving force it transfers when released; the speed and range of flight are affected accordingly. The string is generally drawn as far as possible, but drawing builds up tension within the bow itself, and this can eventually lead to the breaking of the wood. The length of draw is also dependent upon the build of the archer; the greatest distance a man can draw a bow is that between the left hand at the grip and the right ear. Attempts to overcome these two limitations — one technical and the other physical — dictated the development of the bow. The main effort, of course, was put into making a flexible, strong bow which would withstand the repeated tension of drawing to the maximum and being released. It was long before the human limitations could be overcome; only with the revolutionary invention of the crossbow were the problems of drawing solved. In the crossbow, the bow is affixed transversely on a stock parallel to the arrow; drawing is by means of a lever or winch.

If the amount of energy generated by the bow is dependent upon its construction, then the amount of energy ultimately utilized is dependent upon the arrow. A heavy arrow utilizes much of this energy: though it does not fly far it can even penetrate armour. A light arrow has a greater range, but little inertia or striking force. Thus, for a rapid volley, a small bow with light arrows is most efficient; but for powerful shots, a large bow with heavy arrows is preferable. The structure and form of the bows and arrows used by the various peoples and tribes stem both from their technical knowledge and from the use to which the weapons were put.

b. Simple Bow

The simple bow is made of a flexible branch of wood and a string of sinews or fibres. This was the bow of Stone Age man, as depicted in rock-carvings in many parts of the world. Such bows

The crossbow in use by the Ottoman Turks besieging Rhodes (16th century)

were found among most primitive tribes and peoples until quite recently.

A branch of wood, regardless of flexibility, cannot be bent without danger of breaking. Early bow-makers attempted to get round this by making the bow as long as possible; the longer the bow the easier the tension upon the wood during the draw. Simple bows were quite long, averaging five-eighths of a man's height. Even so, they could be drawn only so far; in the best of cases this was up to the chest of the archer. This limitation

is because at first energy builds up gradually within the bow, but toward the end this accumulation is quite rapid. The strain put upon the wood toward the maximum draw is very great and few archers would have had the strength to draw a simple bow to such an extent.

At the beginning of the historical period (around 3000 BC), the simple bow was improved in Egypt, overcoming the above problem. Even at this early stage the simple bow was made recurved — that is, each limb of the

Egyptian archers with bows

bow was curved independently. Since only the grip was thus brought closer to the archer's body, he could in effect make a longer draw — longer by the distance between the grip and the basic curve of the bow. The leverage now available for the draw was increased, and the string could be drawn with greater ease. Such recurved bows proved their worth and were in widespread use in Egypt and the neighbouring lands

during the 3rd millennium and the first half of the 2nd millennium BC.

The simple, curved bow was known in Mesopotamia around 3000 BC. On a stela found at the Sumerian city of Erech (Warka), there is depicted a hunter drawing a very heavy bow. The use of such a bow was undoubtedly very difficult, for not only would it require almost superhuman strength to draw, but also much of the energy generated

Left: The "Lion Hunt Stele" from Uruk; note the spear and heavy simple bow

Arab camel-cavalry using simple bows in battle against the Assyrian army, 7th century BC

within it was wasted in the discharge. Only a small portion of the energy could have been transferred on to the arrow. The artist here may have sought to emphasize the unusual strength of the archer, for he has drawn the string almost to his shoulder. After the initial historical phases, the simple bow went out of use in Mesopotamia, and was replaced by the composite bow. The peoples on the fringes of the Ancient Near East, such as the early Arabs, continued to use the simple bow for many generations, while other peoples, more advanced in military matters, adopted the composite bow.

The bow of the European peoples was always simple. In Greece, the simple bow was in use for many centuries, and we meet it even as late as the 5th century BC. The Greeks seem not to have realized the full potential of the bow, for they were late in developing it to any advanced form. When they did realize its importance, after contacts with foreign armies, they relied upon mercenaries, mainly from Crete, who fought with their own composite bows.

c. Reinforced Bow

An intermediary phase between the simple and composite bows is represented by the reinforced bow. This form

had strips of sinew and wood glued to
the back (the forward-pointing) part of
the bow, enabling it to be bent much
further without breaking. Such weapons
were especially common in regions
where it was difficult to obtain proper
wood for the bow. The Eskimos, for
instance, made bows of bone, reinforced
with sinews to provide flexibility and
most of the strength.

d. Composite Bow

The composite bow represents the
ideal solution to the problems posed by
the simple bow. The composite bow is
constructed of several materials and
fully utilizes the advantageous properties
of each material. The piecing together
of all the parts forms a flexible, strong
weapon which rapidly accumulates
energy from the very beginning of its
draw. It is possible to draw the string
to the maximum and to shoot arrows
a considerable distance. The range of
an especially light arrow shot with a
composite Turkish bow is some 600
yards, but such arrows have little
military value. A volley of arrows shot
from about 400 yards would cause
scattered casualties. The Mongolian
chief Taybugha demanded that his warriors should be able to shoot all their
arrows into a shield 3 feet in diameter
from a distance of 75 yards. This

standard is reasonable, and can be
attained after several years' training.

Turkish bow-makers, who made the
finest weapons of their type, had a rule
in making their composite bows. The
body was made of five plies of three
varieties of wood: the limbs of the bow
were of very flexible wood, and the grip
and the tips were of two varieties of
hard, stronger wood. The tips had to
be very hardy, for their sole function
was to brake the too rapid accumulation
of energy; otherwise the tension would
be too great during release, and the
archer could lose control. The bow-
maker first glued the plies together so
as to form a straight, laminated piece
of wood; in the second stage, he glued
two strips of horn to the belly (inner
part) of the bow, one for each limb.
Next he bent the piece by heating so
that the limbs would form the convex
horns when the bow was strung. Strips
of sinew were then glued to the back;
these were stretched so that the ends of
the bow would bend around and cross
while drying. Again the bow-maker had
to bend the bow under heat till he
achieved its final, unstrung form. In
bracing the bow, the limbs were bent
back by sheer strength, and the string
was put under constant tension, giving
the bow great force. Not only the force
of the taut string but also that of the
limbs, seeking to return to their relaxed

position, made the composite bow a small but very powerful weapon. The composite bow first appears around 2500 BC, on a monument of Naram-Sin, King of Accad; its slightly concave arms and the tips parallel to the string show that this was indeed a composite bow. The small dimensions also point to this. The composite bow was the major weapon of the greatest armies of the Ancient Near East — Egypt and Assyria. The kings of the New Kingdom in Egypt, as well as the rulers of Assyria, are depicted driving chariots and drawing such bows; their enemies trampled asunder and pierced by arrows.

e. Scythian Bow

The most highly perfected composite bow of ancient times was the "Scythian" bow. This weapon was recurved and thus its draw was even greater than the regular, curved composite bow. It was used by the Scythian tribes of the southern Steppes, and appears in Scythian art and on Greek vase-paintings from the 7th century BC on. In the Greek paintings, it appears in the hands of Scythian mercenaries; they are also shown in use by Amazons, the legendary female warriors living on the shores of the Black Sea, and in the hands of mythological heroes, especially Heracles.

The stele of Naram-Sin, King of Accad (*ca.* 2250 BC); note the small complex bow

A mounted Scythian archer, depicted on a Greek red-figured plate (*ca.* 515 BC)

Till not long ago, the "Scythian" bow was not known to have been in use prior to the appearance of the Scythians themselves, that is, in the 7th century BC. In recent excavations at the Mesopota- mian city of Mari, a small stone plaque came to light bearing an incised war scene in the Sumerian style of around 2400 BC. It depicts an archer dis- charging a small recurved bow closely

Battle scene on a stone plaque from Mari; note the Scythian bow and large shield

resembling the "Scythian" bow. This depiction antedates the known "Scythian" bows by nearly two millennia, and the appearance of such a bow there is most surprising. Indeed, on no other Sumerian monument is there any depiction of a bow, leading to the assumption that the Sumerian army did not use this weapon at all. The bow depicted may indicate that the inhabitants of Mari had ties with the peoples of Central Asia — where this type of bow is known to have developed, but at a date apparently earlier than

previously supposed. The difficulties of its manufacture and use may well have lead to the subsequent extinction of this type of bow in Mesopotamia.

3. GASTRAPHETES

A great step was taken forward in the perfection of the bow during the Hellenistic period. Hero of Alexandria, in his *Belopoeica,* one of the principal sources for studying the weapons of the Greco-Roman world, describes the circumstances which brought about the invention of the *gastraphetes,* a form of crossbow. According to him, a way was sought to shoot larger arrows for a greater distance, and to achieve this the size of the limbs of the bow was increased. The drawing of such a large bow proved too much for mere muscle, and thus there was a need for an apparatus to facilitate drawing the string. This new device was called *gastraphetes,* "belly-bow", apparently because it was drawn with the butt of its stock against the stomach. In contrast to most other weapons, we know exactly how and when this instrument was invented: Dionysius I, ruler of Syracuse, had it developed in 399 BC, in preparation for his war against the Carthaginians in Sicily. The historian Diodorus relates that the greatest craftsmen and engineers of the ancient world were gathered by

Dionysius for building up his arsenal.

In spite of this precise information, we know little of the object itself. Not even Hero describes its structure or operation, and we can only guess, basing on Hero's short passage, that it had a large recurved bow affixed transversely to a wooden stock; the string was drawn back along the stock and cocked on some form of release mechanism. The large arrow was placed in a groove along the stock. The advantages of this early crossbow lie in its increased range — some 50 yards beyond that of the ordinary composite bow — and in its heavier missiles, which could pierce armour.

Even with these advantages, it soon became apparent that the weapon was limited by the considerable strength needed to draw it. Further development added a lever to aid in drawing the string back to the release mechanism. The weapon was then cocked like the later crossbows with levers — with the butt against the ground. In its final stage of development, the *gastraphetes* was fixed upon a stand, giving it a range of some 100 yards more than the ordinary composite bow.

The first appearance of the *gastraphetes* on the battlefield was during Dionysius's siege of Motya in Sicily, in 399 BC; he concurrently employed the battering-ram and his new crossbow

against the city, which was unable to withstand the onslaught.

4. ARROWS

Like the bow, the arrow went through a process of evolution. The arrowhead, the operative part of the "bow and arrow", was always made of a hard material — flint or obsidian in prehistoric periods, and copper, bronze or, ultimately, iron in historic times. Its basic form was triangular or leaf-shaped, with a point as sharp as possible for efficient penetration. There was one early form of arrow with a broad, flat head; this appeared throughout the Ancient Near East from Egypt to Mesopotamia at the dawn of the historical period, and was probably intended to cause as wide a wound as possible. This early form seems not to have proved effective, as it was soon abandoned.

During the 3rd and 2nd millennia BC, arrowheads were quite flat and generally leaf-shaped; occasionally they had a central spine. This reinforced the head, giving it the strength needed to penetrate even armour without itself breaking or bending. Throughout this period, arrowheads were tanged. With the advent of the Scythian bow, a socket replaced the tang at the base. Such arrowheads were triangular in section, quite small and very effective.

The arrow shaft was usually half the length of the bow; in any event, longer than the distance between the grip of the bow and the string at its maximum draw. The shaft was made as straight and light as possible, to insure smooth flight. At its tail it generally had several feathers, stabilizing flight to ensure accuracy. These feathers were sometimes fixed at a slight angle, giving a spin to the arrow during flight. The feathers were of such great importance for proper flight that the Persians — excellent archers themselves — called them "messengers of death".

5. CATAPULT AND BALLISTA

In the previous chapters we have seen that the sling and bow are simple devices for concentrating and discharging energy for the purpose of projecting stones and arrows respectively. In all periods people sought to improve these weapons, especially the bow. The real breakthrough in developing a machine for shooting missiles came only in the Hellenistic period. The invention of the ballista and catapult, complex engines powered by elastic tension and shooting large arrows and stones, was perhaps the most significant contribution of the Greco-Roman world to the arsenal of antiquity.

The earliest extant data on these new types of weapons, engines powered by twisted cords, is from around 330 BC, some 70 years after the invention of the crossbow (see above). Hero of Alexandria explains the motive behind the invention of these new devices. The Greeks sought to increase the diameter, and thus the impact, of their missiles to beyond that of even the largest crossbows then available. This led to the need for constructing an engine based on some new principle, and the elastic properties of such materials as hair, sinews and twisted fibre cords were thus utilized. Instead of a composite bow, a heavy wooden frame was built to hold two thick, twisted cords under tension; the cords were symmetrically placed flanking the central shaft of the engine. A wooden limb extended outward from the middle of each twisted cord, and a heavy "string" was fastened to the tips of the two limbs, like a bowstring. This latter was drawn back along the central shaft by a crank, and held cocked by a trigger mechanism. When released, the increased tension of the cords drove the projectile along a groove in the central shaft, and thence into flight.

The principle outlined above was considerably improved upon apparently in Macedonia in the days of Philip II (Alexander's father). Initially, the power of the weapon was rather limited and it could shoot only arrows. Shortly after,

A mobile *ballista,* depicted on Trajan's Column

the ballista made its appearance; this engine hurled stones, and its first recorded use was at Alexander's siege of Tyre in 332 BC.

In the early days after their invention, these elastic-power weapons were not entirely reliable. This seems to be the reason for the extended use of weapons based on the composite bow. Only about 275 BC were the proper proportions calculated for constructing efficient engines of this sort; it was found that the effective range increased considerably with the increase in the diameter of the twisted cords providing the power, and that little gain could be made beyond the optimum diameter. Calculations were made for each weight of missile, resulting in a geometrical formula on the basis of which the optimal diameter of the cord could be determined. This ensured the building of efficient, accurate engines, such as had been impossible before.

The catapult and ballista were the standard artillery in the armies operating in the Mediterranean basin from the mid 3rd century BC on. Though descriptions of these weapons have survived, both in Roman historical writings and pictorially in Roman reliefs, the detailed form and manner of operation are not entirely clear. It appears that the catapult, the smaller of the two types, shot arrows on a rather flat trajectory. The force of the impact of the arrows shot by catapult is demonstrated, for instance, by the wounding of Alexander the Great near Gaza. The arrow penetrated through his shield and body-armour, and entered his shoulder. The ballista was a larger instrument and much more powerful, hurling stones weighting between 70 and 120 lb. on a flat or curved trajectory.

In the 3rd century AD, a heavier and more developed engine was devised, known as the *onager* ("wild ass"). This weapon had a twisted cord arranged horizontally; an arm was inserted into the middle of the twist, with the extremity in the form of a bowl to hold the stone missile. The engine was cocked by crank, drawing the arm back in a vertical arc. When released, the arm lurched forward, hit a padded stop directly above the twist, and discharged the heavy missile ("the wild ass's kick"). On Roman battlefields in England, such stones have been found weighing between 110 and 175 lb.; this engine had a range of some 200 yards.

a. Operation of Catapult and Ballista

The full power of the catapult and the ballista came into play in siege warfare. They were an integral part of the offensive mechanism and assisted the other siege machines which sought to breach the city-walls. Under cover of the large arrows and stones, the besiegers could fill in defensive ditches before the walls, mine the walls, breach them with the ram and even scale them with ladders. The major task of this artillery during the siege was to rid the ramparts of their defenders; it was usually mounted on specially built siege towers. The towers raised the engines far above the ground, often to a level higher than the walls themselves. From this position, the missiles could be rained over a wide area within the city.

A vivid and reliable description of the effective use of the ballista is found in Josephus' *Jewish War* (V, VI, 3): "The engines that all the legions had ready prepared for them were admirably contrived... those that threw darts and those that threw stones were more forcible and larger than the rest, by which they... drove those away that were upon the walls also. Now the stones that were cast were of the weight of a

Reconstruction of an *onager*

talent, and were carried two furlongs and further. The blow they gave could in no way be sustained, not only by those that stood first in the way, but by those that were beyond them for a great space. As for the [besieged], they at first watched the coming of the stone, for it was of a white colour, and could therefore not only be perceived by the great noise it made, but could also be seen before it came by its brightness; accordingly the watchmen that sat upon the towers gave them notice when the engine was let go, and the stone came from it, and cried out aloud... so those that were in its way stood off, and threw themselves down upon the ground; by which means... the stone fell down and did them no harm. But the Romans contrived how to prevent that by blacking the stone, and then could aim at them with success, when the stone was not discerned beforehand, as it had been previously; and so they destroyed many of them at one blow". Often the stone missiles not only sent the besieged soldiers fleeing from the walls, but also damaged the wall proper. Thus, during the heavy Roman bombardment against the city walls of Jotapata (in AD 67), "the violent noise of the stones that were cast by the engines was so great that they carried away the pinnacles of the wall, and broke off the corners of the towers" (*Jewish War* III, vii, 23).

Both the catapult and the ballista were also employed to break enemy formations in the open field. Julius Caesar, for instance, bombarded the coast of Britain prior to landing there, while during the Parthian Wars (AD 62), Cn. Domitius Corbulo prepared rafts by joining boats together and built towers on them to support catapults and ballistae; with these he bombarded the east bank of the Euphrates, causing the Parthians to flee and enabling him to cross the river and form a bridgehead in enemy territory.

Besides arrows and stones, the catapult and ballista were sometimes used to hurl less conventional missiles; it is recounted that during a sea-battle in 184 BC a Roman general showered pottery jars upon his enemy's vessels; the jars contained poisonous snakes which were freed upon the smashing of the jars, spreading confusion and contributing to the victory of the ingenious general! There were also cases of using ballistae to hurl dead bodies of the enemy and carcases of animals into besieged cities, to cause epidemics of disease. These were probably the earliest instances of biological warfare on record.

III DEFENSIVE ARMOUR

A warrior going to battle was naturally vulnerable to the weapons of his enemy, and any wound could remove him from combat. From earliest times, various attempts have been made to protect the warrior, such as by means of some form of impenetrable dress from head to foot, with a large shield in the left hand for added safety. But such a warrior is far from efficient, much of his strength being wasted in merely carrying the weight of his armour. The continual struggle between the need for protection and the desire to rid the warrior of weight and unwieldy dress left its mark throughout the history of development of armour and deeply influenced the choice of materials from which it could be made. In the search for more efficient armour, the usual solutions led to a reduction in protection, that is, covering only the more vital parts of the body. Thus, the head was almost always protected while only seldom were the limbs armoured. The shield, portable and thus readily shifted according to need, was in use almost universally.

Another factor, most important for the development of means of defence, was the nature of the weapons used by the enemy. We have already noted the reciprocity between offensive and defensive weapons, for example the relationship between the mace and the helmet: use of the mace led to the introduction of the helmet which, in turn, led to the obsolescence of the mace as an offensive weapon. The relationship between the axe and body-armour is similar: the hacking axe lost its function with the development of body-armour which, in turn, led to the development of the piercing axe. It was such considerations which led to the extreme variety of armour in various regions and periods.

1. SHIELD

The shield is a portable obstacle placed between the offensive weapons of the enemy and the body of the warrior. Its major advantage over body-armour is its very portability. Its limitations also stem from its nature: if one of the warrior's hands is occupied in holding the shield, only one hand is available for using an offensive weapon. Further, since the weight of the shield must be supported by one hand, it must not be too heavy. The first limitation cannot be overcome, unless a second person holds the shield, but the second can partially be solved by limiting the size of the shield and making it of light but strong materials. This seeking of a balance between weight and protection dictated the form of the shield through the ages.

It is generally assumed that the size of shield in a given army was directly related to the use of body-armour. A warrior whose body was not protected by armour would require as large a shield as possible, while the armoured warrior could make do with a small shield to protect only the face. But this logical formula does not always hold, for there are instances on ancient monuments of groups of soldiers entirely without armour, not even helmets, holding only a small shield. With such meagre means of protection, for instance, the Egyptian army fought all through the 2nd millennium BC. In contrast, there were troops of soldiers, especially in the Assyrian army, who wore fine armour and were protected additionally by a large shield. The rela-

tionship between shield and body-armour is thus rather complex, and generally it is difficult today to determine the precise factors underlying the use of any particular type of protection at any given time or place, or why large or small shields were preferred.

a. Large Shield

Because of its size, the large shield gave the best protection possible, but it was difficult to carry and move about in battle. Even if made not of metal but of wood or leather such a shield was heavy, and all the weight had to be borne by one hand. Its main disadvantage, however, was that it deprived the warrior of a clear view of the enemy before him. These problems can all be seen in even the earliest monuments showing this weapon. The Egyptian soldier carrying the large shield in a tomb-painting of the 20th century BC is indeed protected, from head to foot, but it is doubtful whether he was very effective. It is not surprising that this defensive weapon went out of use rapidly, exchanged for a small shield which gave less protection but enabled the warrior to manoeuvre with ease.

What an individual warrior could not achieve with a shield was, however, realized by troops organized as a phalanx. Thus, we can see Sumerian

An Egyptian soldier (20th century BC), with broad cutting axe and large shield

soldier, and thus the heavy shield would not have been a hindrance; quite the contrary, the almost impenetrable wall of large shields contributed toward the feeling of unity within the phalanx.

Another use of the large shield is known from Greece in the Late Bronze Age (16th–15th centuries BC); at that time two types of large shield were in use, an oblong, tower-shaped shield and a figure-of-eight shield. In profile, the former resembled half of a cylinder, with a rounded top to give protection to the face; the latter was unusual in the history of shields and its shape may have resulted from the manner in which it was made. The figure-of-eight shield was made of a large, oval sheet of hide stretched over two rods bent around so that their ends crossed in the middle. Such a shield was quite convex and the bearer appeared to be standing within it.

A depiction on an inlaid dagger from Shaft Tomb No. IV at Mycenae clearly shows how the warriors of early Greece carried their large shields, with a strap supporting them from the right shoulder, thus leaving two hands free for handling weapons. The large shield was sometimes hung in front and sometimes behind, according to circumstances. But the large Greek shield, even with its relatively light weight, went out of use after only a short time. A connection is sometimes claimed between the disap-

spearmen of King Eannatum marching as a body with quite large shields; but we can also see that they carry their spears with both hands. Thus, either they supported the shields by means of straps over their shoulders, or some of the phalanx bore only shields, and the remainder had only spears. These warriors worked as a team, and manoeuvred as one body on the battlefield. Attack by the phalanx did not demand any specific skill or agility of the individual

pearance of the large shield in Greece and the advent of chariot warfare — a form of war already long familiar in the East (see below). When Greece came up against such "modern" techniques of warfare, it is supposed, the awkward large shield was abandoned for the lighter round shield. It is interesting to note that the large figure-of-eight shield, originating in Crete, eventually took on a ceremonial significance, which led to its continued appearance long after it had lost all military value.

The Assyrian army put the large shield to most effective use. The offensive warrior did not hold it himself, but was assigned a personal shieldbearer. This might seem a waste of manpower, but it did bring to realization the full potential of the large shield. Its protection was especially important for those warriors whose tasks occupied both hands — particularly archers. On the basis of the palace reliefs, we can conclude that the large Assyrian shields were made of wickerwork. The top was often bent back, providing further protection for the head.

b. Smaller Shields

The two ordinary forms of small shields are rectangular and round. Both forms were used concurrently and occasionally supplanted one another. It can be assumed that the use of one or the other form was a matter of local tradition rather than of any considerations of efficiency, for one form has little advantage over the other in any particular function.

The rectangular shield is the older of the two forms, and it served the Ancient Near East from the 3rd millennium BC on. It appears first in Egypt, judging by the hieroglyph for "to fight", which depicts a pair of arms, one grasping a mace and the other holding a rectangular shield. In Egypt, archaeological finds and depictions of shields on monuments do not appear in the 3rd millennium BC, and interestingly they are lacking in contemporary Mesopotamia as well. The Sumerians, who were so outstanding in the development of both offensive and defensive weapons, did not use the small shield; nor did their enemies, the Accadians. Except for the large shield of the phalanx, there is no evidence for the use of any shield whatsoever in the Mesopotamia of the 3rd millennium BC.

An ordinary shield appears in Egypt in the 20th century BC, but it is not clear if this co-existed with the large shield or replaced it. This was rectangular with a rounded top; the type continued to serve the Egyptian army till the end of the 2nd millennium BC, and during this entire period the

The Mycenaean "lion hunt Dagger"; note two types of large shields, long spears and simple bow

Egyptian soldiers besieging a fortified town, 20th century BC; note small shields

Egyptian soldier had no other means of defence. The Canaanites also used a small rectangular shield, but unlike the Egyptians they used it in addition to fine coats of mail.

In the Greek world the round shield was common, though in the vase-paintings of the Geometric period one sees an occasional rectangular shield. In the Roman army, too, the small round shield *(clipeus)* was in use until, in the second half of the 4th century BC, it was exchanged for a large, curved rectangular shield *(scutum)* — the shield of the Roman legionaries, which provided excellent protection originated in the Aegean region, and indeed as early as the 13th century BC it appears in the hands of mercenaries from among the Sea Peoples, alongside the long, straight sword, in the reliefs of Rameses II. The migrations of the Sea Peoples early in the 12th century BC, spreading over Anatolia, the Levantine coast and Egypt, brought a predominance of the round shield to the East. Even so, it should be noted that the round shield appears in the hands of, or hung on the shoulders of, Canaanite warriors in a series of ivory plaques from the early 13th century BC, discovered at Megiddo. Did the Canaanites develop the round shield independently several decades prior to the other armies of the Ancient Near East?

After the round shield had achieved prominence in the East, it became the principal shield in the Assyrian armies during the entire period of greatness of the Assyrian Empire. The round Assyrian shields were mostly flat, with a central handle within and a round, flat boss on the front. The purpose of the boss was apparently to strengthen the shield at the point where the greatest strain was put upon it — at the joint with the handle. There were also other varieties of round shield, such as the convex shield with denticulated edge, or the convex shield with shoulder strap, seen on the back of one of Sennacherib's soldiers while swimming a river.

The round shield occupied a special place in the Aegean world. It appears on the "Warriors Vase" of the late Mycenaean period, circular but with a portion removed from the lower edge. During the Geometric period, the round shield was less used but it later returned to its former position in the form of the *hoplon*, a fairly large shield, about a yard in diameter. It was slightly convex and notably had a metal strip forming a "handle" running within through which the hoplite passed his left arm up to the elbow; the left hand would grasp a short leather strap fixed near the edge of the shield. This manner of holding the shield was an original Greek invention; it is very convenient for bearing a heavy shield, the weight being distributed evenly over the arm rather than concentrated in the hand alone. At time of need, the hand could be released to grasp a weapon — without dropping the shield. The effectiveness of the *hoplon* is proved by its very long lifespan.

The figure-of-eight shield was common for a period in both Greece and the East. We have already noted it in the Mycenaean period, and the Hittites, living in much of Anatolia in the second half of the 2nd millennium BC, used a small shield of figure-of-eight shape, formed by slitting a round shield so as to give it a "waist". This form, removing a superfluous part of the round shield, made it undoubtedly lighter and more convenient for use; however, it never spread beyond Anatolia, at any rate not beyond the limits of the Hittite Empire.

In the Greece of the Geometric period (8th century BC), the "dipylon" shield was common, so named because it is depicted on a group of pottery vessels discovered in the Dipylon cemetery at Athens. This shield was also of figure-of-eight form or, more properly, of hourglass shape; it is sometimes depicted in vase-paintings and figurines of this period in an exaggerated manner — very narrow at the waist and quite wide above and below. Since both the warrior's hands are free in these depictions, it is assumed that the shield was strapped

to the shoulder. This is unlike the Hittite figure-of-eight shields, which were held by a central handle — but was in keeping with the large Greek shields of the 16th–15th centuries BC. We do not know where the dipylon shield originated; it may have been a reincarnation of the large figure-of-eight shields which went out of use hundreds of years previously. This assumption is strengthened by the fact that this shield appears in heroic scenes and is connected with the Greek legendary heroes such as Ajax and Achilles. The dipylon shield, typical of the Geometrical period in Greece, was replaced by the round *hoplon* around 700 BC.

c. Materials for Making Shields

Shields were made of many and various materials, and not necessarily of metal. The reason for this lies in the need to make them as light as possible, so as not to diminish the fighting potential of the bearer. An interesting experiment carried out at Oxford University has proved that metal is not always the material most resistant to penetration. Two shields were prepared, of identical materials and design as ancient shields; one was of leather, made in an original, ancient mould, and the other was of bronze, reconstructed on the basis of the remains of an ancient shield. Both

Greek warriors with *dipylon* shields, riding chariots at a funeral procession; Geometric crater, 8th century BC

shields were round and of similar size. The two were tested against the blows of a large sabre and a spear, and whereas the metal shield was split by the sword and pierced by the spear, the leather shield remained intact. Realizing the relative lightness of leather, we can understand why it was a prime material in making shields throughout history. On the monuments it is easily recognized, for often the surface appears with patches of colour—indications of the natural hair colouring on the hides; these hides were worked so as to leave the hair, the natural pattern serving to ornament the shield. This is seen on the Egyptian shields of the 2nd millennium BC, as well as on the figure-of-eight shields of the early Mycenaeans. The hides were stretched over wooden frames—as can be seen in the shield of Tutankhamon, King of Egypt (14th century BC), which was found in his tomb.

Another important raw material for shields was wood, and wooden shields were often covered with leather for ornament and strength. Such a shield was found in the tomb of Ken-Amon, of the 15th century BC. Wooden shields were also often strengthened by central bosses. Many of the Assyrian shields, as they appear on the monuments, seem to have been of this type. In Europe, from the Greek *hoplon* on, wood was the ordinary material for the shield. The *hoplon* was always strengthened by an outer hoop of metal. Sometimes even the faces of such shields were covered and ornamented with metal, the ornaments (mostly of animal motifs) serving to identify the warrior, whose face was largely hidden by his helmet. In early times each warrior had his own personal symbol, but with the rise of the democracies in the Greek cities, it was the city-symbols which appeared on shields —for example, the owl of Athens or the large letter *lambda* for Lacedaemon (Sparta).

The Roman *scutum* was also of wood. A splendid painted shield found in the excavations at Dura-Europos in Syria shows us how the *scutum* was constructed. It was made of laminated wood, much like modern plywood, to obtain a maximum strength in a thin, relatively light construction. This shield had a metal hoop, as well as a metal boss in the centre. The *scutum* was covered with leather and ornamented with silvered bronze. The shields of the individual units of the Roman army seem to have been painted specific colours, to facilitate identification. A strap within enabled the *scutum* to be hung over the shoulder while on the march.

Wickerwork, either in bundles of cane or woven, was also used in making shields. Wicker shields were very common in the Assyrian army and on the

monuments both large and small ones are shown.

Metal, whether bronze or iron, was used mainly in an auxiliary role—in the strengthening of wooden shields; only seldom was it used as the prime material for an entire shield.

2. HELMET

The helmet has always been a most important piece of defensive armour, since the head is an extremely vulnerable part of the body. Even today its prominence remains, and the modern soldier is helmeted when he enters the field of battle. To give the head maximum protection, helmets have generally been made of metal.

The Ancient Near East has left us but few examples of actual helmets; they were made of rather thin metal sheet which has corroded over the many years in the ground, or they were crushed till they lost all shape. One of the earliest extant examples, however, is perfectly preserved, and it can teach us much of the technical details of helmet manufacturing in ancient times. It is the helmet of a prince, Mes-kalam-dug, of the Sumerian city of Ur, and was found in his tomb. It is made of electrum, a natural alloy of gold and silver. This may not have been an actual war helmet, but it is essentially identical in shape with the royal Sumerian helmets seen on stone reliefs. The helmet is beaten entirely out of one sheet of metal and covers the head and ears. Within there had been a padding of thick cloth, the edges of which were still preserved in place. A series of small holes around the edge indicate that the cloth had been sewn to the helmet, and extended around the outside of the sharp edge, protecting the skin. This helmet is a technical achievement of the highest order.

For later periods, our data on helmets comes almost solely from reliefs and paintings of warriors, rather than from actual objects. Thus, we cannot know whether the later helmets were also made of one piece or of two or more, joined together. A helmet of several pieces is more readily manufactured, though it provides less protection for the wearer, for the joints between the pieces are potentially weak spots. Nor do we know whether helmets continued to be padded within.

The form of the helmet obviously conforms with the contours of the head. It has always been a large metal cap containing the head; this basic cap often rose quite high, with a knob or crest at the top, or was of a slightly conical shape.

This sort of helmet protected the top of the head well, but left two important

Left: Roman legionaries with helmets, *lorica segmenta* armour and *scutum* shields, depicted on Trajan's Column

spots vulnerable—the ears and the nape of the neck. The face, which of course was also vulnerable, remained exposed almost throughout the history of the Ancient Near East. The prime reason for this was the desire to provide maximum vision and free breath during battle. To protect the nape and ears, the rear portion of the helmet was extended downward. The heads of the warriors depicted on the "Standard of Ur" and the Victory Stela of Eannatum are protected by such helmets. This Sumerian helmet, notable for its simple, functional lines, would seem to be one of the most efficient helmets of ancient times. The helmets of the Sumerian city-kings were identical in form, but with the addition of special bulges for the ears and for the knob of hair at the nape. Though providing a defensive advantage, the helmet with extended rear slightly hampered movement of the head and limited hearing. Thus, the simple cap form continued in many variations alongside its more developed offspring. Much later, some of the helmets of Ashurnasirpal's soldiery gave protection to the nape as well, having a sort of armoured neckband depending from the helmet and covering the shoulders.

What is probably the most complex helmet in the Ancient Near East is that of the god-king carved on the "King's Gate" at Bogazköy, the capital of the

Warrior with helmet, socketed axe and dagger, depicted on the "King's Gate" at Boghazköy, Anatolia

Hittite empire (14th century BC). This helmet is slightly conical, with the ears protected by special, wide cheek-pieces, and the nape covered by a suitably shaped piece extending down to the back. These appendages were separate pieces, probably a better arrangement than the one piece of the extended

Sumerian helmets, for it would allow more freedom of movement.

Many of the helmets of the Ancient Near East were ornamented. Some had stripes or studs projecting from the surface; often there was a sort of knob or crest at the top, sometimes in the form of a horizontal crescent, a hook or horns. The most impressive helmets were those with crests of horsehair, plumes or animal tails. None of these ornaments had any defensive value, but they probably served to denote rank or unit. They may also reflect early tribal traditions among the various peoples. In the Assyrian army, various types of soldiers are distinguished by their helmets. Thus, in the army of Sennacherib the spearmen wore round helmets with a plumed, crescent-shaped crest; the javelin throwers wore round helmets with a broad crescent-shaped crest without plumes; the Assyrian archers and slingers had a high helmet; while the auxiliary archers had round helmets with large ear-pieces.

In the distribution of the helmet in the Ancient Near East, we can observe a phenomenon familiar to us from other type of weapons. The pioneers in the development of the helmet were the Sumerians in the 3rd millennium BC, and all the peoples of the Asiatic part of the Ancient Near East used helmets and developed them in many variations.

Throughout the history of Egypt, however, judging from the many extant monuments, the Egyptian army went into battle bareheaded. This may have stemmed from the extreme conservatism of the ancient Egyptians, who often retained early forms of military equipment; but it could well be that the enemies met by the Egyptians were generally so inferior in armament and tactics that little need was felt for developing more sophisticated means of defence. Indeed, we have not even a single example of an Egyptian helmet, a surprising phenomenon in itself.

In the Greece of the Bronze Age there were rather unusual helmets, though all were basically of the round cap type. The materials from which they were made were many and varied. From the Mycenaean period (16th–14th centuries BC), we have several small reliefs depicting warriors wearing helmets made of several rows of small, crescent-like pieces. In the tombs of this period, such pieces were found in large quantities, made from boar-tusks. These helmets, then, are to be identified with the boar-tusk helmets mentioned by Homer in the *Iliad*. This type of helmet was basically a leather or felt cap onto which rows of tusks were sewn. It must have been quite heavy, for 30 to 40 pairs of tusks were needed for a single helmet. This unusual form was undoubtedly

Boar's tusk helmet

From the white dots appearing on the helmets, it would seem that they were made of leather and reinforced with round pieces of metal; this would be one of the few cases in which the helmet was made of a non-metallic material.

A revolutionary change in the basic concept of the war helmet occurred in Greece around 700 BC. The major contribution of Greece as far as the helmet was concerned was undoubtedly the invention of the "Corinthian" helmet; this was made of a single piece of metal, hammered out so as to cover the entire head. There were no separate cheek-pieces, but the long edge at the nape continued almost right round the head. In front, only a narrow T-shaped slit remained open, sometimes with a bar down the middle to protect the nose.

European in origin, for it has no parallel in the Ancient Near East. It disappears around the 14th century BC, after a period of transition during which an all-bronze helmet was in use simultaneously. It is of interest to note that the earliest known metal helmet in Greece was edged with a row of small holes, indicating that it had some form of cloth padding within. Another unusual helmet from Greece appears on the heads of the soldiers on the Mycenaean "Warriors Vase" of the 13th century BC.

Right: Helmet of prince Mes-kalam-dug

Overleaf left: The decisive role played by the complex bow in siege warfare; relief from the palace of Ashurnasirpal, King of Assyria, 9th century BC; note battering ram

Overleaf right: The arms of a Greek *hoplite* — Corinthian helmet, *hoplon* shield and spears, depicted on a black-figured amphora, 6th century BC

Only the eyes and mouth were left slightly exposed. This was the first helmet to give maximum protection even to the face. The Corinthian helmet was a technical achievement of the first order, being hammered out so that its contours corresponded almost exactly to those of the head and neck. Even so, it had certain disadvantages, the most obvious of which was the difficulty of hearing when wearing it; it also limited vision. These minor limitations did not prevent the Corinthian helmet from becoming an integral part of the armour of the hoplite. Such helmets often had ornamental crest of various types.

For over two hundred years the Corinthian helmet was in constant evolution in form. In Chalcis in Euboea, a peculiar variation of this helmet was developed, known as the "Chalcidian" helmet; it, too, was made of a single piece but with an opening for the ears, and with the face much more exposed, the nose guard having degenerated to a mere knob. In this manner the Chalcidian helmet overcame the disadvantages of the Corinthian helmet. In spite of the constant improvements, the Corinthian helmet went out of use quickly during the 5th century BC, making way for other types which had evolved in other parts of Greece. During the 5th century BC the "Thracian" helmet makes its appearance, patterned after the woollen or leather cap so common in northern Greece. The Thracian helmet was a high dome with a short visor projecting the forehead; its cheekpieces were separate, long and wide but leaving a broad opening for the eyes and mouth. This type of helmet was quite widespread and was used in the Macedonian army; it was also used by the Roman army, which developed several variations of it.

3. BODY ARMOUR

Body armour is intended to protect the wearer's body, besides the head, which is covered by the helmet. The making of effective armour is a complex matter, even more so than manufacturing a helmet, for the body armour must allow for free movement of the entire body and limbs. It must be sufficiently pliable, yet must also be hard enough to prevent penetration of the enemy's weapons. Many different materials have been used for armour at various times and places. Heavy leather was undoubtedly one of the earliest important materials. A heavy leather cape extending down to the knees was worn by the Sumerian warriors of Ur; this is the earliest known protective clothing but it was undoubtedly preceded by a long line of more primitive "armour". Such capes seem to have been reinforced with

Left: The statue of the Roman emperor Augustus wearing moulded plate armour

roundlets of metal sewn to them, a forerunner of the later coats of mail. Leather is quite pliable and thus does not hamper the wearer too much; it can, however, be penetrated by an arrow, sword or spear. Leather armour did not go out of use with the advent of metal armour, but appears all through history in periods of technological and economic decline. Thus, the Germanic tribes often wore leather armour up to the beginning of the 2nd millennium AD —a leather tunic and leather breeches, providing both warmth and protection.

Another material sometimes used in protective clothing was quilted cloth. This type of armour put little restriction on movement, but was of limited value as armour. It was used extensively, it would appear, by the peoples of the southern Steppes, notably the Scythians. It was later used in undergarments beneath metal armour.

Undoubtedly the best body protection is provided by a metal garment capable of stopping most ancient weapons. The technical difficulties in preparing a metal garment—one which would allow for free movement—presented a formidable challenge to the ancient armourer, for if it is to provide maximum protection such armour must be both very heavy and very expensive. The necessity of reconciling the characteristics of metal in armour with the need for freedom of

Scale armour of Assyrian archers, 9th century BC; note curved shield

movement led to several basic solutions. Though these problems were identical wherever encountered, the manner in which they were met differed basically in the Ancient Near East and in the West. Thus, the discussion below is divided according to these two worlds, providing a clearer picture of development.

a. Body Armour in the Ancient Near East

In the Ancient Near East the solution adopted almost exclusively was armour

A Canaanite charioteer, his armour pierced between the scales; note also helmet

made up of numerous overlapping metal scales, sewn to leather or heavy cloth, forming a coat of mail. Such armour solved the problem of pliability, but did little to relieve the warrior of the considerable burden involved, for 400–500 such scales were needed to form it. These scales were quite thin, sewn overlapping in horizontal, overlapping rows. There were a very few weak spots — such as the armpit — and these were well known in ancient times: "A certain man drew a bow at a venture, and smote the king of Israel [Ahab] between the joints of the armour" (1 Kings, xxii, 34). This passage emphasizes the chance nature of the shot, for it was certainly quite difficult to aim specifically at such a small point.

Scale armour is a rather sophisticated solution, and we may assume that it was preceded by various lengthy stages of development, nothing of which remains.

The earliest coats of mail known to us are already well developed. The manufacture of the scales was no doubt expensive, and thus such armour would have been reserved especially for those troops whose function necessarily deprived them of the shield. Foremost among these were the archers, who need both hands for the bow; though they usually fought from a long range, they were exposed to the enemy's archery. This was clearly the picture in the Assyrian army of the first half of the 1st millennium BC: select units of archers in the armies of Ashurnasirpal II and his heir Shalmaneser III wore armoured coats reaching to their ankles. Such coats, possible the most developed body armour in the Ancient Near East, were also worn by sappers undermining city walls. In the Assyrian army there were units of archers who did not wear body armour; these may have been auxiliary troops, or possibly foreign mercenaries. Nor did the regular infantry wear armour. The spearmen — the main close-range force of the Assyrian army — were protected by shields. They are often depicted with two crossed straps on their chest, apparently of leather, with a small buckler at the junction, probably of metal, providing some protection there.

The introduction of chariots onto the battlefield produced another class of soldier who, like the archer, needed both hands free of a shield, for the charioteer had to handle both the reins and his weapons. One of the earliest types of armour known to us from the monuments of the Ancient Near East is worn by Canaanite charioteers depicted on the body of the chariot of Thutmosis IV, King of Egypt (late 15th century BC). The scale armour of this early period had a neck-piece of leather, to cover the neck and nape – weak spots left exposed in most subsequent periods. In a temple relief, Rameses II, King of Egypt (13th century BC), appears in full splendour as an archer in his chariot, wearing a sleeved coat of scale armour covering him from neck to below the knees; his Hittite adversaries are similarly dressed. It is notable that the Assyrian charioteers of the 1st millennium BC no longer wore scale armour, possibly because they were protected by shield-bearers riding along with them.

With the development of true cavalry, towards the end of the Assyrian period, a further type of troops needing body armour came into existence. While the charioteer could be protected by a companion adjacent to him, the horseman operated in relative isolation, exposed upon his horse. His one hand was occupied with the reins and the other hand with his weapons. Thus, he had no way of holding a shield, making body-

Assyrian cavalryman with short scale armour

armour imperative. The earliest known cavalry wearing scale armour appears in depictions of the army of Ashurbanipal, King of Assyria (7th century BC).

Though the long coat of mail was an efficient means of personal protection, it was too heavy and too costly. Over the years it diminished to a short tunic of scales. The shortening of the coat of mail was undoubtedly connected with the introduction of the large shield which provided more protection to the archer. The legs were now protected by high boots neck and nape – weak spots left exposed a cloth texture. The increasing importance of cavalry also necessitated changes in body-armour; the combination of coat of mail, short kilt and leggings or boots proved, apparently, to be the most efficient.

b. *Body Armour in Europe*

In Europe the technical solution for metal-armoured garments was quite different from the very beginning. The earliest known body-armour from Greece was made of large plates of metal. The bronze armour found in a tomb at Dendra, not far from Mycenae, is quite surprising in form for the 15th century BC, the same period at which scale armour appears in the Ancient Near East. It consists of two large bronze sheets, one for the chest and the other for the back, forming a cuirass; various strips of metal are joined to them, one for protecting the neck and two for the shoulders. From the hips down, the body was protected by three broad bands of metal, each running around and almost meeting behind. This armour is a milestone in metallurgy and is quite reminiscent of the European knightly armour of 3000 years later. The Dendra armour represents the archetype of most European armour in later periods. The reason behind this extreme difference in character of armour between East and West is difficult to assess. Some scholars attribute it to differences in climate, since metal sheets would hardly be comfortable in the heat of the Middle East. We may note that, though such armour was predominant in Europe, there were periods in which other types were employed, mainly under the influence of contacts with the armies of the East.

Such armour as that from Dendra could not have remained serviceable for long; its considerable weight and complicated structure were not entirely suited to war and, by the 14th century BC, it was no longer in use. Metal armour reappeared in Greece in the 8th century BC, after an interval of some 600 years. We have no direct information on the long, dark period as far as actual armour is concerned, except for the depiction on the "Warriors' Vase" from the end of the Mycenaean period. The warriors on the vase are dressed in tunics with long sleeves and short, closely fitting kilts with fringes. The white dots and strips on these garments have led to the assumption that they were made of leather to which pieces of metal had been sewn—in effect a primitive form of scale armour.

The metal cuirass reappears again in Greece at the end of the 8th century BC. Such armour, made of two sheets of metal, one for the chest and the other for the back, with no protection for the neck, shoulders or lower torso, is known as "bell-shaped" armour because of its outline, which follows the contour of the chest. This armour was used in Greece for two hundred years, and was one of the important elements in the equipment of the hoplite. It is generally thought that the bell-shaped armour, and perhaps even that from Dendra some 700 years older, was derived from the well developed metal technologies of Central Europe, Italy and Gaul—regions where several examples of cuirasses of the same type have been found.

The bell-shaped cuirass began to develop from the mid 6th century BC. Attempts were made to overcome its major disadvantages—the weight of the metal plates and their stiffness. There is evidence that Greek warriors tended to neglect metal armour and return to armour made of quilted cloth, similar to the corselets of the Scythian tribes. But the concept of impenetrable metal armour was not entirely abandoned and the search for a successful form continued. Thus, in the second half of the 6th century BC, a more complex set of armour was devised; no examples of this armour have been preserved, and we cannot know what part of it was made of metal. It seems to have combined the flexibility of cloth with the protection provided by metal, for it consisted of a sort of wide girdle put on from behind and fastened in front. On the basis of the many depictions on painted vases showing such armour, it would seem that the girdle was made of cloth, to which scales were sewn. Thus, this is the first and only appearance of scales in Greece. The girdle of scales terminated in a row or two of leather strips forming a sort of kilt, protecting the lower torso and thighs. Two large

Bronze plate armour from a grave at Dendra

shoulder-pieces, made of leather or possibly metal, were fastened to the fore part of the girdle, completing the armour. Judging by its numerous appearances in contemporaneous vase-paintings, this armour enjoyed a considerable popularity in Greece in the 5th century BC. Such armour allowed the Greek hoplite freedom even to run, something he could never have achieved in the stiff bell-shaped cuirass of old.

This complex armour passed over to the Italian peninsula, where it was greatly utilized among the Etruscans. It was also a favourite in the Macedonian

Greek warriors preparing for battle; note composite armour, *hoplon* shield, Corinthian helmets, bronze greaves; depicted on a red-figured *kylix*, 5th century BC

army. Alexander the Great wore such armour at Issus, judging by the famous mosaic from Pompeii, showing him opposite Darius at the turning point of the battle.

In spite of all the advantages of this type of armour, it did not entirely replace plate armour. In the same period plate armour evolved to the point where it precisely followed the contours of an individual's body. The manufacture of such personal armour required a high technical knowledge, as well as a thorough familiarity with anatomy; this armour almost took on the nature of sculpture. It was fashioned to measure and could be used only for relatively short periods, for no allowance could be made for physical changes. This plate armour, like the complex girdle armour, flourished for quite a time. It, too, reached Italy and has been found in Etruscan tombs of the 4th and 3rd centuries BC. The Romans also adopted it from the Etruscans, and one of the finest examples of Roman armour can be seen on the statue of Augustus Caesar from the Forum in Rome.

After hundreds of years of stagnation in the development of armour, as a result of the efficiency of the complex and plate types, attempts were made under the Roman Empire beginning in the 2nd century AD to make more flexible types of protective clothing, which quickly developed. Up to this period, plate armour was to be found only among the higher officers, while the troops wore a tunic of stiffened leather, sometimes reinforced with metal strips. Beginning in the 2nd century AD, according to the reliefs on Trajan's Column, every Roman legionary was equipped with the advanced armour known as *lorica segmenta,* "segmented armour". This was made of two pairs of small metal plates, one pair covering the upper part of the chest and the other pair the upper part of the back. The remainder of the armour consisted of strips of metal surrounding the lower part of the torso, as well as other strips protecting the shoulders. This is somewhat reminiscent of the early armour from Dendra. The strips and plates were joined together either by thongs or by being sewn to a leather corselet. The entire set of armour was put on from the back and laced up the front.

Soon after, there appeared armour made entirely of strips, with no plates, from neck to waist. For unclear reasons, this latter armour was also replaced, by scale or chain mail; the new armour, however, was neither lighter nor more flexible.

In contrast to the Roman legionary's armour, that of the auxiliaries was quite varied. On Trajan's Column there are depictions of Eastern archers wearing coats of scale mail, in the best Eastern tradition; units of light cavalry, possibly Gallic mercenaries, wearing what appear to be leather corselets; and heavy cavalry, from the Sarmatian tribes living along the Don in southern Russia, wearing scale or chain mail similar to that of the Persians.

From the days of Hadrian onward, cavalry began taking a more prominent place in the Roman army till, in the second half of the 3rd century AD, it became the chief branch. In turn, the infantry declined to the point where the ordinary soldier was second-rate in both fighting quality and equipment. The infantry gradually shed its armour, first exchanging metal for leather and, subsequently, abandoning even that. In contrast, the armour of the cavalryman was improved upon. Fighting from horseback not only demanded armour, but also was one of the principal factors in bringing about its further development. Since the cavalryman did not have to bear all the weight of the armour him-

Roman legionaries wearing strip armour, depicted on a base of Antoninus Pius's Column

self, heavier and more complex suits could be devised. Armour was the most costly item in the soldier's kit, and thus armoured cavalry gradually became the preserve of the upper classes. It thus came to play a role in preserving the class structure of the ancient world, and can be considered as one of the symbols, and possibly even one of the foundations, of class division within the Byzantine world and in Europe in the Middle Ages.

IV THE CHARIOT

The war-chariot was one of the most complex and developed weapons serving the ancient warrior. It can be defined as a mobile platform, mounted on wheels and motivated by animal power. The exploitation of animal power enabled the speed of the attacking force to be increased several-fold. Chariots could appear swiftly on the battlefield, manoeuvre freely and retreat in haste.

To put the chariot to its most advantageous use, it had to be engineered so as to provide an ideal compromise between two opposites. On the one hand, the strength and speed of the horses drawing it had to be exploited to the maximum, and thus the body had to be made as light as possible. On the other hand, a light chariot could carry only one warrior, and was thus less suited for battle, for two hands were not enough to control the horses, fight and protect the body all at the same time.

This required a second person, leading to a larger and heavier vehicle. A larger chariot, for driver-warrior and shield-bearer, also required facilities for storing weapons and "ammunition"—bow-cases and quivers. Such chariots necessarily put more strain upon the horses, reducing their speed. The search for a mean between these two opposing factors led to continual efforts toward developing a more advanced chariot—both by using lighter yet strong materials and by improving the form and function of its various components.

The considerable technical knowledge and economic means required for improving the chariot were possessed by only the most wealthy and advanced nations in antiquity. Indeed, the strength of an army in ancient times would often be measured by the number of chariots it could field. Thus, inscriptions of the first millennium BC found in China note a "nation of a hundred [or a thousand] chariots". Ahab, King of Israel (9th century BC), contributed 2000 chariots to an allied army of kings opposing Assyria, and this number exceeded that of the chariots of all his allies combined. Such a large body of chariots is highly indicative of the strength of the kingdom of Israel in that period.

1. EMPLOYMENT OF THE CHARIOT

The exact role of the chariot in warfare is a point of dispute among scholars. It is sometimes held that it was used for direct assault upon the enemy, thus providing a smashing blow on the battlefield proper. Such an assault, especially against infantry, could have heavy psychological impact. But it is also maintained that the chariot was used only in the initial phases of battle. When the opposing forces were still far apart the chariots moved at the front, providing long-range fire against the enemy. Distance was kept so as not to endanger the horses, but the display gave vent to the desire for pomp and glory upon the battlefield. After this had been fulfilled, the chariots fell back, to serve for evacuating wounded, for retreat or for pursuing the retreating enemy.

Both of the above theories are well based. The first, for instance, regards the raising of the front panel on the early chariots as a protective measure during close battle. In contrast, the second theory notes that a horse provides a large, convenient target at close quarters, and in falling would bring the entire chariot down, encumbering the battlefield and thus leading to utter chaos among the attacking forces.

The weapons employed by the charioteer can aid in attempting to ascertain the role of the chariot on the battlefield in the various periods and places. The appearance of the bow—the weapon with the greatest range in ancient times — as the principal weapon of the Egyptian and Assyrian chariots would seem to favour placing the chariot in the "softening-up" stages of battle, for the bow had little function in close-up, face-to-face combat. The depictions of chariots running over enemy troops, in Egyptian or Assyrian art, appear to be a symbolic means for showing superiority, rather than being realistic. On the other hand, the appearance of such short-range weapons as the spear would seem to place the chariot in the midst of the mêlée.

Thus, the chariot probably did not have a single, simple function at all times and places. Just as its form developed, so did its role on the battlefield.

2. THE EARLIEST WAR VEHICLES

Wheeled vehicles for use in war are encountered in the first half of the 3rd millennium BC, employed by the armies of the Sumerian cities. The Sumerians early recognized the advantages of such weapons in warfare, though the vehicle they developed could hardly be called a chariot; its cumbersome nature made it more of a battle-wagon. In spite of its weak points, it was widely used in

Sumer, and much detailed evidence remains on its construction and use.

The Sumerian armies used two types of battle-wagon, one lighter and two-wheeled, and the other heavier and four-wheeled. Both types were clumsy and quite obviously left much to be desired. The conflict between speed and mobility, on the one hand, and convenience of riding and fighting, on the other hand, was far from solution. These wagons were harnessed to onagers (wild asses), not the strongest of draught animals, and thus their speed was quite slow. To gain power, the Sumerians would harness teams of four onagers.

The structure of these battle-wagons did little to ease the burden placed upon the onagers. The wheels were solid, made of three planks joined by wooden clamps. The tyre was also of wood. Such wheels revolved on a long axle, often twice as long as the width of the wagon proper. The body had a wooden base-board, with low sides and a higher front panel; it was open behind, with a special platform for the warrior at the rear. The weapon of the warrior was the javelin, and a quiver was attached to the front panel.

The weight and awkwardness of the Sumerian battle-wagon did not prevent it from taking part in the actual fighting, as is indicated by the "Standard of Ur", which shows such wagons in various stages of attack.

This early appearance of the battle-wagon is limited strictly to the Sumerian city-states. There is no evidence for its use anywhere else. Thus, the Sumerian battle-wagon was a local development which disappeared along with its inventors, and had no influence on or connection with the chariots which later developed in this part of the world.

3. THE TRUE CHARIOT

The chariot first appears in the 16th century BC, in a quite well developed form. We know nothing of its ultimate origins—where it was developed, by whom and in what process, for it surely underwent a lengthy process of development prior to its sudden appearance upon the stage of the Ancient Near East.

This new chariot, revolutionary in both its light, stable form and its harnessing of horses (rather than onagers), was always two-wheeled, indicative of its light nature; further, the wheels were spoked rather than solid. The light weight led to the second major characteristic of the new chariot—the moving of the axle from the centre of the body to the rear edge. The rear position of the axle, besides placing the load squarely on the horse's shoulders and reducing the strangling effect on the throat, largely prevented overturning. The harnessing, however, was still quite in-

Horse-bit from Tell el-'Ajjul, Palestine, 18–17th centuries BC

efficient, placing undue discomfort upon the horses.

a. The Spread of the Chariot

The war-chariot appeared in Canaan, Egypt and Greece at about the same time. In all three regions, the chariots held in common several of the characteristics noted above—the use of horses, spoked wheels and light body. In all three areas, the earliest examples had axles at the centre of the body whereas subsequently the axle was moved to the back. Scholars generally agree that the new type of chariot reached Egypt through Canaan, but its ultimate origin is still an open question. The great similarity between the Canaanite–Egyptian chariots and those in contemporary Greece would point to some common source, outside Canaan.

The Central Asian Steppes—famous as a homeland of the wild horse—are often suggested as the place of invention of the horse-drawn chariot. In the period under discussion, the late 17th and early 16th centuries BC, waves of nomads swept out of the north over the lands of Central Asia. Among these peoples were the Kassites, who devastated the Early Babylonian and Hittite empires, forming a mighty kingdom of their own. It is generally assumed that it was these tribes who introduced the light, horse-drawn chariot—a weapon which may well have been the factor responsible for their battlefield successes and their ability to conquer so extensive an area. Offshoots of these tribes reached Canaan via Syria, and Greece via Anatolia. Other such groups moved eastward into China and southward into India—also thus introducing the horse and chariot. So far, however, archaeology has failed to find remains of a Steppe culture of the first half of the 2nd millennium BC sufficiently developed to be credited with the invention of the chariot — one of the greatest revolutions in ancient warfare.

b. The Egyptian Chariot and the Canaanite Chariot

The earliest Egyptian chariots known to us are also the lightest in weight; the body is a scant wooden framework and the wheels, with only four spokes, are mounted on an axle at the back of the body. In tomb-paintings we see depictions of Canaanites presenting tribute to the Egyptian kings, including chariots of a type identical with the Egyptian chariot. This indicates that the Egyptians probably derived their light form from the Canaanite type.

In Egyptian battle-scenes, chariots are shown with six-spoked wheels; the increase in number of spokes may indicate a heavier chariot, possibly for two persons. However, Canaanite chariots depicted in battle against Thutmosis IV (late 15th century BC) bear two warriors but have only four spokes per wheel. In the typical Egyptian battle depiction, often only the king appears in a chariot, always with the reins tied around his waist while he draws a bow. In reality, the king certainly was not so exposed to enemy archery, but we cannot know exactly how many persons regularly accompanied him in his chariot, though there was at least a shield-bearer to protect him. Indeed, a chariot crew of archer and shield-bearer does appear in the instances where non-royal chariots are depicted, such as on the famous painted chest of Tutankhamon (1361–1352 BC).

In the depictions of the Canaanite chariots, there is no consistent number of spokes; most wheels have four, but some have six spokes. It is not clear how many persons rode in the Canaanite chariot, for they mostly appear overturned. In the six-spoked Canaanite chariots the axle is often located at the centre of the body, indicating that the Canaanites were not able to overcome the technical difficulties of harnessing the heavier, six-spoked chariots.

c. The Aegean Chariot

The earliest appearance of the chariot in the Aegean world is in the depictions on tombstones and several art-objects found in the Shaft Graves at Mycenae, dated to the 16th century BC. These chariots have four-spoked wheels with axles located at the centre of the body. Thus, they seem to be derived directly from the area of origin, rather than via Egypt as has been suggested. In contrast to Egypt and Canaan, where the chariot underwent a process of development, in the Aegean world it retained its initial form down to the 8th century BC. This seems to indicate its relative unimportance in Aegean warfare. After the decisive stages of conquest by the invaders from Anatolia over the southern parts of Greece, during the 16th century BC, the war-chariot lost whatever prominence it had previously held, the local terrain possibly not being considered

Assyrian slave battle chariots; note the large wheels

suitable for chariots. This disregard for the chariot is fully indicated in the Homeric epics, which reflect the traditions of the second half of the 2nd millennium and the first centuries of the 1st millennium BC. Chariots were used as a means of reaching the field of battle, as well as in funeral processions of great warriors, as seen on jars of the Geometric style, of the first half of the 1st millennium BC. On the battlefield proper, the warriors dismounted and fought on foot; in none of the epics is the chariot used in the heat of battle.

In spite of the conservative form of the Aegean chariot, the body did undergo some development. In the earliest chariots, it was square with low sides woven of canes or made of leather; later, the body was square with a rounded addition behind, of unknown function, and another type had rounded sides.

In the 8th–7th centuries BC, the chariot dropped from use altogether in the Aegean world. In the Classical period, infantry was predominant and no Greek battle-chariot is known.

d. The Assyrian Chariot

The chariot was the prime assault force of the Assyrian army in the first half of the 1st millennium BC. We do not know the source from which the Assyrians derived their knowledge of chariot-building, and a gap of many centuries separates their products from even the latest of those of the Sumerians. Under

Reconstructed Egyptian chariot

the Assyrian empire, repeated attempts were made to improve the chariot, mostly seeking to develop a form sufficiently sturdy to bear an increased crew but still able to manoeuvre without exhausting the horses. Thus, the diameter of the wheels was increased, and in the days of Ashurnasirpal II, they were two-thirds of the total height of the chariot, whereas under Ashurbanipal, some 200 years later, they were about eight-tenths of the height. The thickness of the tyres was almost doubled, the number of spokes increased from six to eight. Such large wheels as the latter are indicative of heavy chariots capable of bearing a considerable load; indeed, in Ashurbanipal's army the chariots were manned by a crew of four—driver and archer in front, and two shield-bearers behind.

In the form of the body and pole, no significant changes took place. Several Assyrian kings added what appears in the reliefs as a large, elongated ellipsoid, between the tip of the pole and the rim of the body; it is not clear, however, whether this was flat or somewhat thickened, nor how it functioned.

The Assyrian chariot left its imprint upon the chariots of all the surrounding nations – the Aramaeans and Cypriots in the West, and the Persians in the East.

e. The Chariot in Fringe Areas

The chariot seems to have reached the Far East directly from the Steppes of Central Asia. Very well-preserved chariots have been discovered in the tombs of the Shang Dynasty in China (14th–13th centuries BC). Their light chariots were built of wickerwork; the wheels were large with numerous thin spokes, and the axle was positioned at the centre of the body. The harnessing of the horses was similar to that found in the Ancient Near East.

The chariot reached Central and Northern Europe by way of Anatolia and possibly Greece. A depiction of a chariot on a stone plaque from the tomb of a tribal chieftain in Southern Sweden (around 1200 BC) witnesses its use in Northern Europe as early as the late 2nd millennium BC. In Europe, the war-chariot continued in use long after it had gone out of use in the Near East.

Literary sources relate that the Gauls and Samnites nearly vanquished the Roman army at Sentinum in 295 BC with the aid of a thousand chariots. Chariots appear to have been used last by the Celts of Britain—as late as the conquest of their island under Claudius in AD 43. The Roman army never employed the chariot in war, although chariot racing was a popular sport in Rome. Still within the Roman period the cavalryman came fully to replace the charioteer on the battlefield.

4. THE DISAPPEARANCE OF THE WAR-CHARIOT

During the 1st millennium BC, in the Ancient Near East, Greece, Central and Western Europe and the Far East, the chariot gradually declined from its position as prime battle vehicle, giving way to the mounted horse. The cavalryman held a decided advantage over the charioteer, for the chariot could operate only in specific topographical conditions. We may ask why true cavalry was so late in making an appearance on the battlefield. It is often held that the degree of domestication of the horse was a decisive factor and that early in that process horses were too small to bear up under the load of a warrior in battle. Breeding led to larger, stronger strains, providing horses suitable for cavalry use.

ILLUSTRATION SOURCES

Israel Museum, Photo David Harris, P. 15. British Museum P. 12; 27; 30; 31; 43; 48; 80. Cairo Museum P. 16; 18; 24. Israel Department of Antiquities and Museums P. 11; 19; 70; 89. A.C.L. Bruxelles P. 23. Metropolitan Museum of Art, Rogers Fund P. 25; 47; 91. Alinari P. 26; 34; 57; 68. Hirmer Fotoarchiv, Munich P. 33; 66. Archaeological Receipts Fund, Ministry of Science, Greece P. 36; 63; 72. Massada Press P. 37–39; 73–76. Rainbird Ltd., London P. 40. Bibliothèque Nationale, Paris P. 45. Baghdad Museum P. 46. Louvre Museum, Paris P. 50; 92. Ashmolean Museum P. 51. Drawings by Ofra Kamar P. 52; 82. Kunsthistorisches Museum, Wien P. 83.

INDEX